William Bledsoe Philpott

The Sponsor Souvenir Album

and History of the United Confederate Veterans' Reunion, 1895. Patriotic poems,

war songs, romantic incidents, biographical and historical sketches

William Bledsoe Philpott

The Sponsor Souvenir Album
and History of the United Confederate Veterans' Reunion, 1895. Patriotic poems, war songs, romantic incidents, biographical and historical sketches

ISBN/EAN: 9783337103552

Printed in Europe, USA, Canada, Australia, Japan

Cover: Foto ©Thomas Meinert / pixelio.de

More available books at **www.hansebooks.com**

Flags of a Nation that fell.

THE SOUTHERN CROSS.
BATTLE FLAG DESIGNED BY
GEN. JOSEPH E. JOHNSTON.

BATTLE FLAG ADOPTED BY THE CON-
FEDERATE CONGRESS IN 18—

THE STARS AND BARS.

FLAG ADOPTED BY THE
CONFEDERATE CON-
GRESS IN 18—.

THE

Sponsor Souvenir Album

AND

HISTORY

OF THE

United Confederate Veterans' Reunion,

1895.

PATRIOTIC POEMS, WAR SONGS, ROMANTIC INCIDENTS,
BIOGRAPHICAL AND HISTORICAL SKETCHES.

EDITED BY

WILLIAM BLEDSOE PHILPOTT.

ILLUSTRATED.

HOUSTON, TEXAS:
SPONSOR SOUVENIR COMPANY.
1895.

PREFACE.

THIS VOLUME has been very hastily prepared, and approaches but approximately the conception of the author, who hopes in another edition to more nearly realize his ideal.

The Album is its own excuse for its existence.

The omission of any U. C. V. Officers, or of any Sponsor of a U. C. V. Camp, the editor begs to say is no fault of his, but must be attributed to the tardiness or indifference of those not represented.

For valuable assistance in compilation, I am largely indebted to my friend and associate, Professor Robert F. Smith of the Texas Agricultural and Mechanical College; and I desire to divide with him any measure of praise which may be accorded the work.

Mr. S. A. Cunningham, editor of the *Confederate Veteran*, of Nashville, Tennessee, has placed me under obligations for numerous courtesies for which I desire to to thank him sincerely.

For appreciated courtesies, I also desire to thank: General George Moorman, Mrs. Mollie Moore Davis and Dr. Joseph Jones, of New Orleans; Editor R. M. Johnson, Dr. H. V. Philpott, Dr. E. P. Daviss, Mr. B. R. Warner and Mrs. Rosine Ryan, of Houston ; Mr. Guy A. Collett, of Austin, Texas : and Mr. Foster Forte, of Waco, Texas.

Credit is due the publishers, the Terry Engraving Company of Columbus, Ohio, for beauty of illustration and excellence of typographical work.

THE EDITOR.

SEPTEMBER 10, 1895,
HOUSTON, TEXAS.

Dedication.

This Volume, the maiden effort of one whose youth has made him stranger to war's alarms, is offered as an humble tribute to the virtue, beauty, and patriotism of the Southern women, whose deeds of sympathy, mercy, and loving kindness in times of war and carnage, can never be adequately told in song or story.

To Miss Varina A. Davis, known to the Confederate Veteran as Miss "Winnie" Davis, the youngest child of the great Confederate Chieftain, the idolized daughter of the Confederacy, the embodiment of those womanly graces conspicuous in the fair daughters of the Southland, which have made the Southron the gallant, chivalrous, gentleman that he is, and the Southern soldier the knightliest that ever drew sword in defense of home and country, this volume is most respectfully and lovingly dedicated.

William Bledsoe Philpott.

MISS VARINA A. DAVIS, ("WINNIE" DAVIS).

"DAUGHTER OF THE CONFEDERACY."

To The Departing Confederate Soldiers

One by one they pass away,
  Cross the river one by one;
And the shadows of to-day
  Darken the departing sun.
'Tis a hero falling, seeking
  In eternity sweet rest,
While his country's tears are reeking
  Sorrow's passion rends the breast
Of the chivalry and beauty
  South of Dixie's magic line.

One by one the ranks are thinning,
  And a comrade falls to sleep.
Death invades our sanctum, winning
  Jewels rare we fain would keep;
Jewels from the Southern cross,
  Tried by fires of deadly war,
Who shall recompense our loss?
  Will their spirits from afar
Whisper us some consolation,
  Minister at freedom's shrine?

by Smith Johnson,
Tyler, Texas.

STONEWALL JACKSON.   JOS. E. JOHNSTON.   ROBT. E. LEE.

NOTED CONFEDERATE GENERALS.

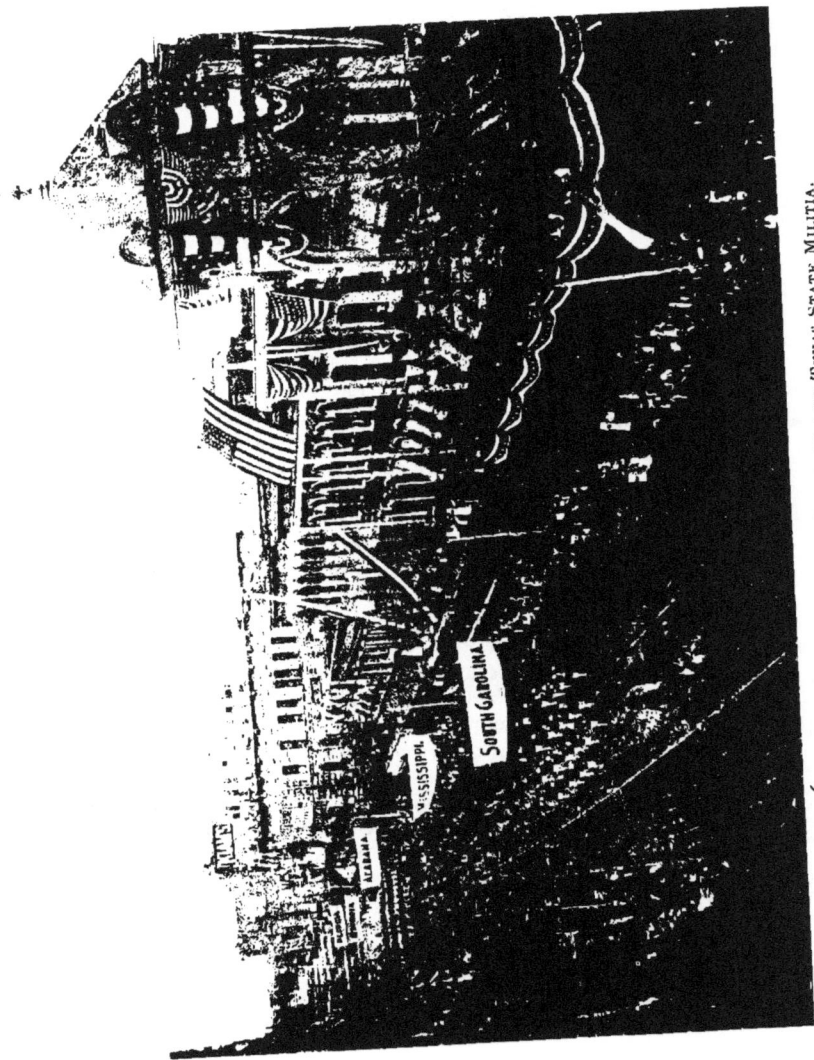

Street Parade in Houston—U. S. Regulars and Texas State Militia.

THE REUNION.

For who could, e'en in bondage, walk the plains
Of glorious Greece, nor feel his spirit rise
Kindling within him? Who, with heart and eyes,
Could walk where Liberty had been, nor see
The shining footprints of her deity,
Nor feel those God-like breathings in the air,
That mutely told her spirit had been there?
                                    —Moore.

THOSE young sons of the South, and there were thousands of them, who visited Houston during the United Confederate Veterans' reunion of 1895, could nowhere have learned loftier lessons of patriotism, nowhere have seen brighter exemplars of the highest type of manhood; no where have spent time more pleasantly and profitably than in mingling with and listening to the men whose courage and devotion upon the field a third of a century ago won the plaudits of an admiring world; whose wisdom and patriotism have since built up the waste places of the South and caused to blossom as a garden the country ruined by war's devastation.

The prime objects of the United Confederate Veterans' Association are the meeting and intermingling of friends and comrades of the war time and the preservation and promulgation of the true history of the causes leading up to the strife, the manner in which it was carried on through four bloody years, and the salient features of the succeeding period of reconstruction.. The historical part, to the end that succeeding generations of Southrons may know the reasons that animated their ancestors; that they may appreciate their courage upon the tented field, their patriotic devotion in accepting the stern decree of war, and in the face of mountainous obstacles, carrying the commonwealths of their section once again to the front rank of the sisterhood of states. The *raisons d'etre* of the organization are more fully set forth in the following excerpt from the constitution adopted at the Houston meeting:

Article 1. The objects and purposes of this organization will be strictly social, literary, historical and benevolent. It will endeavor to unite in general federation all associations of Confederate veterans, soldiers and sailors, now in existence or hereafter to be formed; to gather authentic data for an impartial history of the war between the states; to preserve relics or mementoes of the same; to cherish the ties of friendship that should exist among men who have shared common dangers, common sufferings and privations; to care for the disabled and extend a helping hand to the needy; to protect the widows and the orphans, and to make and preserve a record of the services of every member, and as far as possible of those of our comrades who have preceded us in eternity.

What more commendable object could organization have than to promote social intercourse among comrades whose ranks are being rapidly thinned by the destroying hand of time, than to promote the truthful chronicling of the acts of a period of such vital importance to the life of the nation? For no gain, save that of pleasure; for no ambition, save that the truth be told! The sordid desire for financial gain and the self-wish for personal political preferment are so almost universally to the fore at all large gatherings in these days of broadening avarice and narrowing ambition that it is particularly and peculiarly pleasing and refreshing to attend a meeting of men whence all such thoughts are banished and each speech and action has for its object the promotion of social pleasure or the encouragement of patriotic endeavors.

In its personnel the meeting was the most notable that has gathered in the South since the surrender at Appomattox, embracing the representative brains and bravery, sense and chivalry, of that section of this country which has been wont, in all its history, to hold first place in field and forum. The roll of those present embraced names not only illustrious in battle, but which, in the thirty years of peace that have followed the last sound of war's loud alarm, have been written high upon the reunited nation's scroll of honor.

With such men met for such object, what wonder that the three days of the meeting should be full of the most intense sentimental interest and freely interspersed with the most electrically dramatic speech and action?

What splendid types of men the leaders among these veterans are!

John B. Gordon, the soldier and courtier, the statesman and orator, graceful wearer of the highest honors his native state has had to bestow.

Stephen D. Lee, able general in time of war, chivalric gentleman always, now giving his life to the instruction of the youth of his adopted state.

Lawrence Sullivan Ross, boy commander upon the frontier, dashing brigadier, as knightly a man as ever laid lance in rest, having, like Gordon, worthily worn the highest honors his people had to bestow, and now, like Lee, giving the ripened years of his manhood to the guidance of the youth to that high standard of manhood of which he is the splendid exemplar.

Cabell, who knew only fight when the foe was afield; Law, who hides behind the modesty of a woman the courage of a crusader; Waul, whose proud boast it was that no enemy rested foot for twenty-four hours on Texas soil; Shelby, the bold raider, whose business was war and whose pleasure was fight; Evans, as gentle in peace as he was courageous in battle; Boone, who talked of the duty "we owe our maimed comrades" as though he had not been unlimbed in one of the most gallant charges of the great struggle—these were there, and a hundred others, distinguished officers, whose lives in war and peace are fittest for the copying of the youth of the land.

> "Good knights and true as ever drew
> Their swords with knightly Roland,
> Or died at Sobieski's side
> For love of martyred Poland;
> Or knelt with Cromwell's Ironsides,
> Or sung with brave Gustavus,
> Or on the field of Austerlitz
> Breathed out their dying aves."

There were also present by the thousand, and no less worthy examples of the courage and manhood of the South, the private soldiers of the lost cause. They were the men who, with no thought of self-advancement, with neither epaulette nor star beckoning on, fought because they deemed it their duty to fight, offering their lives upon a thousand battle fields as willingly and as cheerfully as did ever crested knight in tale of mediæval romances.

From every battle field of the war had these veterans come.

Heroes were there who had stood upon Bull Run's successful field with Jackson when he asked for ten thousand men with whom to march into Washington; who were with Bragg at Chickamauga and Albert Sidney Johnston at Shiloh; who breasted the storm at Gettysburg when Pickett's division marched through the hail of leaden death to all but the topmost point of Cemetery Ridge; who refused to follow Lee at the Wilderness, but who swept back Grant's columns after their beloved commander had been forced to seek safety at the rear; who, with Joe Johnston, for months doggedly threw themselves across Sherman's pathway and vainly sought to obstruct his march to the sea; who fought with Ross and Estes, with Forrest and Hood, with Gordon and Longstreet, and Beauregard, and Wade Hampton, and Jeb Stuart, and the Hills, upon a hundred fields of bravery and blood; who, ragged and hungry, but still defiant and undaunted, laid down their arms at Appomattox, and, accepting war's stern decree, returned to desolated homes and deserted firesides to do citizens' duty to their restored country in patriots' way.

Well may the record of their lives be an inspiration to succeeding generations, filling their minds with high ambition, swelling their hearts with a patriotic desire to carry forward the work so nobly begun, until their section shall be the most advanced of the whole country in all those material and intellectual elements that distinguish the highest civilization.

Nor have the lessons been lost, for while the sturdy sons of these noble sires enjoy and appreciate the enterprise and prosperity of the "New South," they do not forget or undervalue the glory and the chivalry of the old, and more than all other names, they venerate those of the men, living and dead, whose bloody footprints marked the path of patriotism from Fort Sumter to Appomattox, whose stainless swords wrote in flaming characters the deathless record of a nation that was doomed to die, who, when all resources had failed, and to further fight would have been but reckless folly, accepted defeat with the same courage that had won them so many victories, and returned to their homes to repeat in peaceful pursuits the heroic devotion to duty they had shown in war.

There was no word said, no act done in all that great gathering, which smacked of perfidy to the terms upon which the Confederate soldiers accepted their restoration to citizenship; nothing to which the most caviling critic could take exception. Every word of sorrow spoken was for the brave who fell in the great struggle, every sentiment expressed was full of a broad and patriotic spirit which took in the whole country. "Old Glory" was the name by which was designated the flag before whic 1 the Southern cross went down in blood, and the only sectional feeling expressed was in the assertion that the South had given to it the broadest stripes and brightest stars. A short excerpt from a speech made in the convention by Rev. J. William Jones, "the fighting parson" from Virginia, and more nearly "unreconstructed," perhaps, than any other living Confederate, shows the regard in which the flag of the common country is held:

"Old Glory!" said he, "why should we not march under its folds and glory in its lustre? It was designed from the coat of arms of our Washington; 'The Star-Spangled Banner' was written by a Southern man, when Southern troops had just won a glorious victory on Southern soil. Our Taylor, our Scott, our Jefferson Davis, Joseph E. Johnston, our Robert Edward Lee, our Magruder, our Albert Sidney Johnston, our Stonewall Jackson, our Beauregard, and others of that brilliant galaxy of Southern officers, bore it on the most glorious fields of Mexico and planted it upon the walls of the Montezumas."

And the feeling of the Confederate veteran for the highest types of the Northern soldier and statesman found expression in the following quotation from the eloquent oration of General Peyton A. Wise, of Virginia:

By the side of Hendrick Hudson's flowing river, just away from the busiest hum of the most multitudinous city, just on the skirts of a progress seemingly the most splendid because it is the most selfish, rises apace an erection, the free gift, without gleaning from the public stare, of a free people, lifted above their progress, stealing away from their hum, to be grateful to the savior of the people's union. An illustrious soldier and president is to be canonized in the affections of a people every way composite, and the expression of that affection is to be a heaven-kissing monument. Let Grant's monument rise, the higher the better, the sooner the more fitting. He deserved it. He was not composite; he was genuine, unadulterated, unlimited Saxon pluck and pertinacity, fighting always in the splendid way in which God gave him to fight for the thing he believed in and loved. He deserved it, even from us, if only because in the moment of his tirumph he mounted no triumphal car, but said, "Let us have peace," and acted it. But for him and dead Lincoln, what would have become of the Union, even after the war?

No word of bitterness, no expression of regret! If any virtue outshines the courage of the Southern soldier in time of war, it is his patriotic devotion to the whole country in time of peace.

FIRST DAY'S SESSION.

The reunion was in session three days, the meetings being held in a splendid new auditorium, designed and constructed especially to accommodate large gatherings of the kind.

It is not the purpose of this work to give a detailed account of the business transacted at these meetings—the daily press of the country did that upon each successive day, and full official minutes have been published. The scope of this work is intended to embrace only the most notable features, to put in enduring form only those scenes and incidents which, though full of heart-interest, have no proper place among the things set down in the official reports.

The first striking incident of the opening day's session was the reception given General Gordon, when that battle-scarred hero appeared before the assembled multitude for the first time. When his tall, erect form was seen moving across the stage, the eyes of thousands of veterans recognized him, and "Gordon!" "Gordon!" "Gordon!" was the cry from all parts of the great building. Every veteran rose to his feet: hats and handkerchiefs were waved and the "wild rebel yell" shook the walls. For several minutes the ovation continued, and no stranger or alien present could have doubted the esteem in which the Confederate soldier held the man whom General Peyton A. Wise described as "that bow of promise to every man in the Confederate army who feared that danger might come too near Lee, and who has lived to show that a man surcharged with the most loving memories of a past that was filled with the glories and the liberties of his section, may be the most orderly, the most faithful, the most devoted servant of the whole country."

Shortly after General Gordon's arrival the meeting was called to order and great enthusiasm was again evoked by a welcoming speech of rare grace and eloquence by Governor Charles A. Culberson, the handsome and boyish-looking chief executive of Texas.

After a further speech of welcome by Hon. John T. Browne, mayor of the city of Houston, General Gordon rose for the response, and again for several minutes he had to stand in silence before such a demonstration of devoted love as few men have ever won from their countrymen. When at last he was allowed to speak, he did so with that fervid eloquence, that grace of diction and nobility of sentiment that are so large a part of the man.

The preliminary speeches over, the meeting went straight to business, only to be interrupted, almost at the outset, by one of the most extraordinary scenes that was ever witnessed at any gathering. General Stephen D. Lee had but begun reading the report of the historical committee, when Miss Winnie Davis, youngest daughter of Jefferson Davis, entered the building and was conducted to the stage. She was recognized instantly and the vast audience arose to greet her. It was not intended that she should be presented just then, but nothing else would do, and General Gordon, leading her to the front of the stage, said:

"Comrades, I present to you the daughter of Jefferson Davis—the daughter of the Confederacy—our daughter."

Then the applause was redoubled, and for ten minutes nothing could be heard save the huzzas which it seemed must surely shake down the walls of the building. The manner of the recipient of this magnificent ovation from an assemblage that numbered the leading men in war and peace, from the Potomac to the Rio Grande, from Mason and Dixon's line to the sea, is thus described by a writer in the Houston Post:

And how sweetly, bravely and self-composedly she bore the trying ordeal. Modestly, gracefully, with remarkable self-control, every moment perfect mistress of herself, she stood before that vast throng, smiling upon them, bowing right and left and front, stirred with emotion that showed itself in flushed cheek and kindling eye, enjoying the homage paid her for her dear father's sake, yet without the least show of self-consciousness. Those present were as completely captivated by the sweet graciousness of her personal bearing and demeanor as they had been thrilled by the sound of her name. It was a scene never to be forgotten by any one who enjoyed the privilege and pleasure of witnessing it.

The veterans could not suppress the emotion that welled up within them at sight of the daughter of their beloved chieftain—the child born to him while the war was in progress—the daughter of the Confederacy—and they clapped their hands and shouted and waved their hats and shook out the folds of many a bullet-scarred battle flag, "while down their bronzed cheeks, like rivulets through sand," the great tears coursed.

It was many minutes before General Lee could proceed with the historical committee's report, and even when he did go on, it was amid the greatest confusion and frequent interruptions from those who, at the sight of Miss Davis, could not suppress their enthusiasm. This report was the most important matter considered by the meeting, for it covered the very kernel of the nut which the United Confederate Veterans' Association was organized to crack. It was an able, elaborate and analytical paper, discussing in succinct language many points upon which the South has been made to suffer by Northern writers of history, who have not only misrepresented the causes which led to the war, but have also misstated the actual occurrences thereof—such as victories won by either side, relative numbers engaged, and other details. The gist of the report may be gathered from the following extracts:

In nothing has the South suffered so much at the hands of the writers of school history, as in the treatment of the subjects of state sovereignty, nullification, slavery and secession. Since the success of Northern resources over Southern arms in the civil war, it has been the practice of Northern writers to isolate the period of the war and either uphold the specific acts of the South in withdrawing from the Union as a political crime, using as a term of reproach the term rebellion, or to infer from the fact that Southern independence was not maintained, that secession was morally wrong. The facts of American history rob the reproach of its sting when it shows that the foundations of our present government were laid in secession, the states moving in the matter, virtually seceding from the perpetual union under the articles of confederation, that the structure of American independence was upreared in rebellion, that subsequently every section of the country has at some time threatened to secede. In reference to the question of nullification, it was not one of the Southern states that alone proposed it, but it originated in the North, where many of the states, by legislative enactment, nullified the constitution of the United States, especially with respect to the fugitive slave law, that the whole country, and not the South alone, was responsible for slavery, the system prevailing in the North as long as it was found profitable; that the slave trade was made possible only by New England vessels manned by New England crews. The true cause of the war between the states was the dignified withdrawal of the Southern states from the Union to avoid the continued breaches of that domestic tranquility guaranteed but not consummated by the constitution, and not the high moral purpose of the North to destroy slavery, which followed incidentally as a war measure. As to the war itself and the results of the war, the children of the future would be astonished that a people fought so hard and so long with so little to fight for, judging from what they gather from histories now in use, prepared by writers from the North. They are utterly destitute of information as to events leading to the war. Their accounts of the numbers engaged, courage displayed, sacrifices endured, hardships encountered, and barbarity practiced upon an almost defenseless people whose arms-bearing population was in the army, are incorrect in every way. A people who, for four long years, fought over almost every foot of their territory, on over two thousand battle fields, with the odds of 2,864,272 enlisted men against their 600,000 enlisted men, and their coasts blockaded and rivers filled with gunboats, with 600 vessels of war manned by 35,000 sailors, and who protracted the struggle until over one-half of their soldiers were dead from the casualties of war, had something to fight for. They fought for the great principle of local self-government, and the privilege of managing their own affairs, and for the protection of their homes and firesides.

While the South would detract not an iota from the patriotic motive and endeavor of those opposing them, she intends that the truth of history shall be written by a sympathetic and friendly pen, to give her credit for what our ancestors did, and for what was done by the South in the war between the states. Also, to chronicle the results of that war and its effects upon the South and upon our common country. * * *

A true history is now desired. The war between the states and its issues are things of the past and are committed to history. The duty of patriotic citizens in every part of our common country is to strive with citizens of every other section to promote the progress and glory of our grand country in working out its destiny. Secession and slavery are decided forever against the South. It makes no matter now who was to blame and how plainly the right of a sovereign state to withdraw from the Union is established by legal right or by the construction of our highest court, the matter is finally settled. When Jefferson and Madison construed our constitution in one way and Washington and Hamilton in another, surely there was ground for their descendants to honestly differ in construing the constitution. Now, the facts of history must be made to speak for themselves and equal and exact justice must be done everywhere. The flag of our country is not the peculiar heritage of any section or part of this Union; each of its many sections can claim its part and its proper share of the honors. Let us be honest everywhere; let us tell the truth, even to the record of the war between the states and the causes leading to it, and the facts after the war. There is honor and glory enough for all; for North, for South, for East, for West. The South and its descendants to this present time are willing to abide by the true record impartially put into history. Your committee is pleased to report that a growing interest in this matter of a true history of the United States is apparent at the South, as also at the North; that the time has at last arrived when truth can be told, listened to and digested without the passions and prejudices of the past. The histories written by Northern historians in the first ten or fifteen years following the close of the war, dictated by prejudice and prompted by the evil passions of that period (and generally used in the schools) are unfit for use, and lack all the breadth, liberality and sympathy so essential to true history, and, although some of them have been toned down, they are not yet fair and accurate in the statements of facts. Many of these histories have an edition for use in Northern schools and another of the same history for use in Southern schools, toned down and made to pander, as is supposed, to Southern sentiment.

What is needed is a history equally fitted for use North and South, and divested of all passion and prejudice incident to the war period. Until a more liberal tone is indicated by Northern historians, it is best that their books be kept out of Southern schools. The veterans of the Northern and Southern armies now look at the issues for which they fought more dispassionately, and there are many pointers indicating a more liberal and a fairer view of the motives and aspirations of the two sections in the great struggle.

It is therefore important that the Southern people be aroused and take steps to have a correct history written, a history which will vindicate them from the one-sided indictment found in many of the histories now extant. The love of a common country is now invoking a spirit of truth, concession and fairness in reviewing the causes which led to the war, and in discussing the conduct of the war and its results. It is conceded that both sections had right on their side as they construed the constitution, and certainly the valor displayed is evidence that they were sincere and believed they were right. The movement is assuming

WINNIE DAVIS AUDITORIUM WHERE THE REUNION MEETINGS WERE HELD.

the best and most permanent form, and the demand is growing for truth, not self-adulation and disparagement of the other side, not crimination and recrimination. The public sentiment is well tempered and patriotic, as attested by the tone of the press, by the increase in the number of historical articles in magazines and periodicals and in publication of such books as "The South, Constitution and Resulting Union," by Rev. Dr. J. L. M. Curry, of Virginia. The Northern tone is much more liberal. The government is continuously publishing official reports and other material throwing light on all matters of difference.

Yet with all this the South was conquered in war, and if Southern veterans who are living, and their descendants, do not look to their own vindication by sympathetic pens, the record of history will contain many errors and false indictments against the South, which have originated with Northern writers with that partiality for their section which is evident from the coloring of history from the landing of the first colonists in Virginia to the present time. Most of this awaking of interest in the desire for a true history of the United States is due to the action of the Confederate veterans, the judicious and liberal tone of their proceedings directed to vindication and to manly assertion of broad sentiments, and the consciousness of high patriotic motives and intent in defending principles they knew to be right.

And after failing in manly and heroic conflict to sustain those principles, in restoring their allegiance to one common country, feeling it to be their country, feeling that their ancestors did a prominent and large part in building and developing it. While some of us may conscientiously think it is not the union of states first formed, that it is a new and more centralized, stronger union, and not the one our fathers established; yet such as it is, it is now the best government in the world; it is our government, and it has our admiration and love. The love of a common country, which should animate every patriotic citizen, demands a fair and impartial history to transmit to our descendants a proper respect and regard for a common ancestry.

At the conclusion of the reading of the report, and after its unanimous adoption, opportunity was given those who desired, to shake hands with Miss Davis, and for more than an hour the members of that great gathering filed past her in a steady stream, neither of her hands ever being released by one before another was ready to press it in token of the love and esteem in which her name was held.

General Gordon, too, was forced to hold an impromptu reception, and his hands were grasped by thousands, many of whom had seen him in the battle front when, with undaunted courage, he flung his gallant legions against the serried phalanx of an outnumbering foe.

The evening session was given up chiefly to a discussion of the need for a new constitution, the matter being referred to a committee for consideration and report, and the convention adjourned early to give the veterans an opportunity to enjoy a concert arranged for their entertainment. The program was made up of songs and recitations, the numbers chosen being from those of the war period, and the excellent renditions were greatly enjoyed.

SECOND DAYS' SESSION.

The meeting of the veterans on the second day was, perhaps, the most enjoyable of all, for it was characterized by such a display of the wonderfully eloquent oratory for which the South is noted, as is seldom given men to enjoy. After the new constitution had been read and adopted, the committee in charge of the Davis monument fund made a report, and General Cabell, in speaking to it, touched a chord in the breast of Dr. J. William Jones, which set his nerves to thrilling and loosened his tongue to the utterance of a most passionate burst of patriotic eloquence.

As soon as the committee report had been disposed of the convention decided to go into the selection of a place for the next reunion, and General Peyton F. Wise, of Virginia, took the stand for the purpose of placing Richmond in nomination. The name of Wise carries with it the aroma of oratory, for its bearers have been among the most eloquent sons of the Old Dominion, and much was expected from the veteran who bore it and spoke for Richmond. But even those who knew him best were not prepared for the gem of oratorical effort that dropped from his lips with such electrical effect.

Other eloquent speeches followed—that of Mayor Davis, of Kansas City, audacious, witty, original; of General Clement A. Evans, speaking for Atlanta; of General Law for Charleston, and of a number of those who seconded the nomination of each city, forming, altogether, a feast of eloquent utterances that was thrilling in effect.

The ballot showed a majority for Richmond over all, and the choice of the capital of the Confederacy was made unanimous.

At night the veterans were again entertained at the auditorium, the program being made up chiefly of tableaux, in which scores of young ladies from all the Southern states took part. The brilliant lights, the bright costumes and the lovely faces of these fair daughters of the South, the beauty represented being of every conceivable type, made the pictures presented upon the stage radiantly beautiful and never to be forgotten by the beholders, while the shouts and applause that greeted each successive scene showed the esteem in which Southern chivalry holds Southern loveliness.

THIRD DAYS' SESSION.

The session of the third and last day was given up chiefly to the selection of a commander-in-chief and department commanders. The only contested position was that held by Lieutenant General W. L. Cabell, of Texas, commander of the trans-Mississippi department. The friends of the gallant General T. N. Waul, also of Texas, urged him for the place, and it took a roll-call of the Texas camps to decide between him and General Cabell. The latter, however, proved the stronger, and his re-election was made unanimous.

Of the newly created department of the Army of Northern Virginia General Wade Hampton was elected commander and General Stephen D. Lee was re-elected commander of the Army of the Tennessee, both by acclamation.

The scene attending the re-election of General Gordon as commander-in-chief was remarkable beyond description. He was placed in nomination by Major J. N. Stubbs, of Virginia, and his nomination seconded by General Stephen D. Lee, who moved to elect him unanimously and by acclamation.

The veterans did not wait for the question to be put, but immediately all arose, and the cheering lasted several minutes. General Gordon was deeply moved, and as he stood upon the platform and faced the remnants of the grandest army that ever drew sword in cause of right, and witnessed the outpouring of their love, tears flowed freely down his cheeks, and his emotion almost overcome him. When quiet had come again he said:

Only the searcher of all hearts knows the debt of gratitude your action awakens in this heart. I would rather have my place in the hearts open to me to-day than any honor this earth has to bestow. The proudest epitaph that can be written upon my tomb when your hands shall lay me to rest, is, "Here lies a Confederate soldier." God bless you, my fellow-soldiers, and make me worthy of this honor.

In keeping with the broad spirit of patriotism which characterized all the acts and utterances of this great meeting, was the splendid greeting given Colonel E. T. Lee, a federal soldier, now secretary of the Shiloh Battle Field Association. Colonel Lee, who is, by the way, a splendid type of sturdy manhood—tall, erect and firm of carriage—explained the object of his association as being to furnish a common place of meeting for the veterans of both armies, where all would feel equally at home. He invited the Confederate veterans to the Shiloh field, not as strangers or as guests, but as soldiers exercising their rights, for they had the right. Other officials of the association, he said, had been in the Confederate army, and it was the intention of all connected with it to make Shiloh, once the scene of the exercise of the most splendid valor of both sides, now the home of both.

Colonel Lee's speech was greeted by tremendous applause, and the reception given him filled him with emotion.

Immediately following the speech of Colonel Lee, General Gordon caused to be read a cordial letter of greeting from General J. M. Schofield, of the United States army, who had been for some days in the city. The letter was full of a patriotic sentiment that embraced the entire country in its scope, and its reading was greeted with great cheering.

INTERIOR VIEW OF WINNIE DAVIS AUDITORIUM.

A communication from Charles Broadway Rouss, of New York, an ex-private in the Confederate army, now a very wealthy man, and almost totally blind, was read by the secretary.

Comrade Rouss proposed a plan for preserving in some central locality the archives of the Confederacy and such historical data as has been or may be gathered from time to time, so that the historian who wants facts, or the future Southron who wants to know the truth of his ancestors, may be conveniently accommodated. He held himself ready, he wrote, to head the subscription for this purpose with a donation of $100,000 whenever a properly matured plan should be agreed upon.

The proposition of Mr. Rouss, accompanied by his offer of such a generous donation, was received by the veterans with great demonstrations of appreciation.

The last minutes of the meeting were given to a scramble for flowers, which showed, in a manner, the esteem in which the city of Houston was held by the visitors. General Gordon said two great baskets of Cape Jasmines had been sent—one to the convention and one to himself; he laid "both at the feet of the veterans." In a few moments each flower ornamented the lapel of a soldier's coat, and a thousand veterans declared they would preserve as mementoes the buds whose fragrance was not more sweet than the memory of the hospitality of the people of Houston.

At 12:45 Friday, May 24, the fifth annual reunion of the United Confederate Veterans adjourned sine die.

SOCIAL FEATURES OF THE REUNION.

THE society functions, given mostly in honor of the daughter of the great Confederate chieftain, were among the many pleasant accessories of the greatest of Confederate reunions. The monster reception at the auditorium and the daily morning receptions to the sponsors, in Armory hall, were admirably planned and carried out by the ladies' reception committee, headed by Mrs. J. C. Hutcheson, wife of the congressman of the First Texas district. But these public functions have been often described elsewhere, and it is the intention to embrace in this sketch some of the various teas, receptions, etc., given by private individuals.

AT JUDGE MASTERSON'S.

On Wednesday evening, May 23, Judge James Masterson and his daughter, Miss Masterson, gave a very elegant card reception in honor of their guest, Miss Varina Davis, daughter of the late president of the Confederate states, Hon. Jefferson Davis, at Judge Masterson's stately mansion, on Main street. The large parlors and hall were crowded from 9 to 12 o'clock at night. The elegant toilettes of the ladies, the faultless dress suits of the civilians, the glittering uniforms of officers, and the crush and jam everywhere, reminded one vividly of state receptions at Washington in the height of the season. Houston's four hundred and representatives of the four hundred of many other Southern cities were there in force, swelling the number to seven hundred or more. Miss Davis was, of course, the center of attraction. She is elsewhere described in this volume, but no words can give an idea of her charm of manner, her winning smile, her soft musical voice, her marvelous personal magnetism, a heritage from her illustrious father. Personally, Miss Davis strongly resembles her mother, both in face and figure, but mentally she is very like her father. Her manner, also, is like his, and his irresistible fascination.

23

Miss Masterson stood next her guest of honor and was assisted in receiving by Mrs. William M. Rice, Mrs. William H. Palmer, Mrs. Seabrook W. Sydnor and Mrs. Rector, of Austin. The younger ladies, who, dressed in charming shepherdess costumes, assisted in the supper room were, Miss Rector, of Austin; Miss Dale, of Tennessee; Miss Root, Miss Justine Franklin, Miss Nealie Wilson, Miss Bessie Hill and Miss Bentley.

MR. AND MRS. RICE.

Mr. and Mrs. William M. Rice threw open their elegant and spacious apartments in the *belle etage* of the new flats, corner of Texas avenue and Travis street, Thursday morning, from 11 to 1 o'clock, in honor of Miss Davis. During and after the hours named the throng into and out of the rooms was tremendous. Here, as at the other receptions given during the week, many persons prominent in the late war were objects of attention and interest. General John B. Gordon, of Georgia; General Wheeler, of Alabama; General Nelson, of Alabama; General Cabell, of Dallas, Texas; Mrs. Lucia Polk Chapman, a daughter of General and Bishop Leonidas Polk, of Louisiana; Mrs. Charlotte M. Allen, of Houston, aunt of the hostess, a pioneer settler, aged ninety years, and Mrs. P. L. Hadley, another pioneer Houstonian, aged eighty-eight years, who was devoted to the Confederate cause.

Miss Davis occupied the place of honor in the line formed in the front parlor, with the hostess on one side and Mrs. John H. Reagan, wife of the Confederate postmaster general, and only survivor of President Davis' cabinet, on the other. Others assisting Mrs. Rice were: Mrs. Charlotte M. Allen, Mrs. P. L. Hadley, Mrs. Walter Gresham, of Galveston; Mrs. Stone, of Galveston; Mrs. Louise Cleveland, of Galveston; Mrs, J. C. Hutcheson, Mrs. Thomas R. Franklin, Mrs. William D. Cleveland, Mrs. Charles S. House, Mrs. S. K. McIlhenny, Mrs. Julius Kruttschnitt, Mrs. William Baker Turner, of Houston; the Misses Willis, of Galveston; Miss Nelson, of Alabama; Miss Ashe, of Dallas, Texas; Miss Leovy and Miss Bobb, of New Orleans; Miss Root, Miss Cleveland, Miss Hutcheson, Miss Masterson, Miss Carson, Miss Porter, Miss Franklin, Miss Bessie Hill, Miss Dillingham, Miss Simpson, Miss Delgado. Miss Cargill, Miss Tina Cleveland, Miss Mildred Hutcheson, Miss Usher, Miss Ballinger, Miss Bryan, Miss Opal Smith, Miss Hunter, Miss Clemens and others, of Houston.

HONOR TO JUDGE AND MRS. REAGAN.

Mr. and Mrs. Charles Bein gave a delightful informal reception Friday morning, from 11 to 1 o'clock, at their handsome residence, 1904 Main street, in honor of the most distinguished citizen of Texas, Hon. John H. Reagan, and his lovely wife, who were guests of Mr. and Mrs.

Cotton Exchange

U.S. Post Office

Harris County Court House

Market Scene

The Hero of San Jacinto 1836

City Hall and Market House.

HOUSTON.

Bein during the reunion. Although greatly fatigued by a rapid succession of social episodes, Miss Davis honored her father's cabinet officer and faithful friend by her presence and was as much sought after as though she had just arrived in the city.

At this, as at all the receptions, flowers were artistically and lavishly used in decoration, and elegant luncheons or suppers were handsomely served; and like the others, also, the visitors went way up into the hundreds of cultured, refined, agreeable women and men. Among those assisting Mrs. Bein in receiving and caring for her guests were, her mother, Mrs. Bobb, and her sister, Miss Bobb, Mrs. Lucia Polk Chapman, of Louisiana; Mrs. William M. Rice, Mrs. Charles S. House, Miss Root, Miss McKeeon, Miss Leovy, of New Orleans; Miss Bangs, of St. Louis, and Miss Usher. The younger ladies were stationed in the dining room and were most attentive to the guests.

A BUFFET LUNCHEON.

This was the informal and most delightfully social way in which Mrs. JuliusKruttschnitt chose to give Miss Davis a quiet, pleasant hour or two free from the crushes which were inevitable at the larger functions that preceded it. Miss Leovy and Miss Rogers, who were Mrs. Kruttschnitt's guests during the reunion, assisted the hostess in her pleasant duties. The old Ben Botts homestead has been the scene of many pleasant affairs since it became the residence of Mr. and Mrs. Julius Kruttschnitt, but never to better purpose than on this bright, unstudied occasion. Miss Davis had opportunities to show the remarkable talent for entertaining for which she is justly so much admired. The luncheon was delicious, and served from the buffet, and conversation rippled and sparkled as in the olden days, so that the hours from 1 to 3 in the afternoon were winged.

HONOR TO "THE FENCIBLES."

Mr. and Mrs. T. W. House gave a very elegant reception to the Fort Worth Fencibles, of which their daughter, Miss Mary House, was sponsor, Thursday evening, from 9 to 12, at their beautiful home, on Louisiana street, and it proved one of the most agreeable features of the Reunion. The whole lower floor was thrown open, brilliantly lighted, and made most lovely by the feathery foliage of exquisite palm trees, reaching nearly to the ceiling and raised in the fine conservatory attached to the house. Smaller palms adorned the stairway and were placed in groups in every room. Miss House received her guests in the drawing room to the right, assisted by her maids of honor, Miss McDowell, of Bastrop; Miss Root, Miss Cleveland and Miss Porter, of Houston, and by Miss

Emily Taylor, Miss Mildred Hutcheson, Miss Tina Cleveland, Miss Usher, Miss Nannie Usher, Miss McKeever, Miss Belle Moore, of Bastrop; Mrs. Walter Howze, Mrs. Berry W. Camp and Mrs. John Shearn.

The Fencibles were out in full regimentals and made a very fine appearance. Diehl's string band and the Fencibles' brass band alternately made the air vocal with concord of sweet sound. Mr. Joe H. Eagle made the address of welcome, to which the captain of the company eloquently responded. A superb supper was served amid much cheerful interchange of talk and merry laughter, while music from without shed its joyous influence over all.

Among the guests present, in addition to those already mentioned, were: Mrs. Edward M. House, of Austin; Mr. and Mrs. Charles S. House, Mr. and Mrs. William J .Hancock, Mrs. McDowell, of Bastrop; Mrs. Tankersley, Mrs. Haven, Misses Cooper and Clark, of Fort Worth; Miss Bronson, of Victoria; Miss Elliott, of New Orleans; Miss Lubbock, Miss Justine Franklin, Miss Mamie Lubbock, Miss Batcher, Dr. Lamkin, Messrs. Berry W. Camp, Philip Carson, W. D. Cleveland, Jr., Harcourt, Curth, John Shearn, Scott, Walter Howze, Henry Howze, Frank Howze, Abbott Cockrell and others.

— · ·

Mr. and Mrs. L. T. Noyes gave a large and brilliant reception in the parlors of the Capitol Hotel, Friday evening, in honor of the Washington artillery, of New Orleans. The host and hostess received their visitors at the door of the east parlor and were assisted by Mrs. Lawrence Sullivan Ross, wife of ex-Governor Ross, and Mrs. Sims, of Bryan; Mrs. Hearne, of Austin; Mrs. J. C. Hutcheson, Mrs. B. F. Weems, Mrs. Charles S. House, Mrs. Rosine Ryan, Mrs. W. D. Cleveland, Mrs. W. H. Garrow, Mrs. T. U. Lubbock, Mrs. R. C. Giraud, Mrs. Robert Rutherford, Mrs. Robert Brewster, Mrs. Seabrook Sydnor, Mrs. Louise Cleveland, Galveston; Mrs. Chapman, Mrs. Bronson, New Orleans; Mrs. Ida Tyler, Miss Harn, sponsor for Texas; Miss Nelson, sponsor for Alabama; Miss Herrington, Miss Opal Smith, of Georgia; Miss Willie, of Galveston; Miss Scruggs, of Dallas; Miss Rutherford, of Austin; Miss Cleveland, Miss Lubbock, Miss Mamie Lubbock, Miss Hutcheson, Miss Mildred Hutcheson, Miss Franklin, Miss Tina Cleveland, Miss Bryan, Miss Hartwell, Miss Hennie Price and Miss Kirkland.

A HAPPY EPISODE.

The band which came with the Washington artillery was borrowed for the occasion from the Continental Guard, of which Charles W. Drown is captain. Now, Captain Drown is an old friend of Mr. and Mrs. W. B. Chew, and charged the band to be sure and give them a serenade while in Houston. On Saturday the drum-major, Mr. Adolph Berendsohn, who was acting leader in place of Mr. John Wunch, who could not leave home, asked Mr. Chew if it would be agreeable to him to receive a serenade, as Captain Drown had directed. Needless to say, it was agreeable, both as a musical treat and a souvenir of his old friend. Mr. Chew and his lovely wife but half enjoy pleasures unshared by their friends, so the neighbors were notified, and by 2 o'clock the handsome hall and parlors were well filled with friends. The band appeared promptly at 2 P. M., and stopped at the front gate, while two beautiful numbers were played. The players were then invited on to the broad veranda and served with champagne, lemonade and cake, as were also the assembled guests. Then the music was resumed and the audience held spellbound for an hour, after which Mrs. Chew presented the band with an exquisite floral harp of sweet peas and maiden-hair fern. The drum-major was presented with a beautiful bouquet and the band left, much delighted with this specimen of Houston hospitality.

FOR GOVERNOR CULBERSON.

The young governor of Texas was the recipient of many pleasant hospitalities during his stay in Houston reunion week. Among the most delightful of them was an elegant dinner given to himself and his chief of staff by Mr. and Mrs. Charles S. House, at their elegant home, on Main street, Tuesday evening. Superb roses, jasmines and ferns made bits of gay color in the daintily tinted drawing room, and soft mandolin music floated down from an alcove at the head of the massive stairway. The feature of the dining room was a broad dining table covered with white satin damask and a white lace scarf extending down the center from end to end. Tall cut-glass vases held maiden-hair ferns and a large bowl of the same costly material in the center of the table was filled with sweet peas. Silver and crystal ware reflected back the light from the chandelier overhead in a thousand prismatic rays. The viands served were worthy the charming accessories of the table; the company was congenial and appreciative, and the evening went into the past laden with pleasant memories. Those present were: Mr. and Mrs. Charles House, Governor Charles A. Culberson and General Mabry, guests of honor; Mr. and Mrs. Edward M. House, of Austin; Mr. and Mrs. William D. Cleveland, Mrs. William M. Rice, Mr. and Mrs. Berry W. Camp, Congressman Bell, of Fort Worth, and Hon. J. R. Fleming, late of San Antonio.

THE FLOWER PARADE.

Notwithstanding the rain, about fifteen beautifully decorated carriages drove through the principal streets of the city Wednesday evening, carrying charmingly gowned women and children, with a sprinkling of

U.S. GOVERNMENT WORK at MAGNOLIA PARK

MAGNOLIA PARK AVENUE

VIEWS

BUFFALO RIVER—LOOKING SOUTH FROM PAVILION

MAGNOLIA PARK,

MAGNOLIA

HOUSTON.

distinguished men. The planning and execution of the beautiful feature is due to Mrs. William M. Rice, who very properly headed the procession with Miss Davis. Her carriage was decorated on the outside with magnolias and the harness and interior were traced in Cape Jasmines. Mrs. J. C. Hutcheson's carriage was done in pond lilies and golden butterflies; Mrs. W. D. Cleveland's in pale pink roses; Mrs. T. W. House's in wistaria; Mrs. Charles S. House's in pink poppies and pale blue ribbons; Mrs. John H. B. House's in La France roses; Mrs. S. B. Dick's in yellow chrysanthemums; Mrs. Pressley K. Ewing's in red roses; Mrs. Henry S. Foz's in white roses and green ribbons. Others taking part in the parade were: Mrs. W. A. Childress, Mrs. H. F. Ring, Mrs. Charles S. Wigg, Mrs. William Baker Turner, Mrs. J. T. D. Wilson and Mrs. Isaac Baker.

OTHER RECEPTIONS.

Mrs. P. J. Willis, of Galveston, gave a reception to Sterling Price Camp, at their headquarters, in the Capitol Hotel, which was a very *chic* affair.

An impromptu reception was held at the Capitol Hotel in honor of General J. M. Schofield, United States army, at which all the Confederate generals and a number of ladies were present.

The Alabama Camp gave a reception to their state sponsor, Miss Nelson, and her maids of honor, Miss Mary Harralson and Miss Lida Nelson, which was largely attended by the Alabamians now living in Houston.

The Tennessee contingent gave a reception in honor of the state sponsor, Miss Carrie Montague Jennings, and her maid of honor, Miss Fannie Millard Sparks, Friday evening, in the parlors of the Capitol Hotel, which was a most delightful affair.

Dr. and Mrs. Byers gave a charming tea in honor of the Texas Woman's Press Association, Friday evening, at their quaint colonial home on Bagby street.

The Misses Taylor gave a dance in their father's residence, on Crawford street, in honor of their guests, Miss Fowler, Miss Dora Fowler, Miss Brooks and Miss Bailey, of Paris, Texas, on Monday evening, which was a very pretty function.

AFTERNOON TEA.

The non-arrival of Mrs. Mollie E. Moore Davis was, of course, a great disappointment to the large concourse of people who filled the handsome residence of Mr. and Mrs. S. K. McIlhenny Thursday afternoon, from 4 to 7, yet regret at the absence of our Texas poetess (who has become a New Orleans story writer) did not prevent the assembly from being a very merry one. Iced tea, deliciously flavored with lemons, mint and other nice things, was served with cake in the rooms opposite the drawing rooms. This was one of the pleasantest affairs of the week.

WHEELER'S SURRENDER.

One of the most prominent features of the great reunion was a public reception tendered General Wheeler and his charming and accomplishd daughter, Miss Annie, at the Light Guard Armory, given under the direction of Terry's Texas rangers. General Wheeler was escorted from their headquarters on Main street, and on reaching the armory was met by his daughter, where a bower of lovely women were guarded by a detachment of brave and courteous gentlemen.

Their presence was announced by Captain T. U. Lubbock, aided by Postmaster G. B. Zimpelman, of Austin, and Captain R. Y. King.

For two long hours, to the strains of martial music, cordial greetings were exchanged and a happy time was had. It is estimated that at least five thousand of the leading gentlemen of Houston graced the occasion by their presence.

The gallant old general never felt prouder of his daghter, and the man who had led armies on a dozen battle fields of the great war was captured at last by his old Texas rangers in Texas.

The "Old Bee Hunter," as the boys used to call him, felt his condition and appreciated the demonstration of kindness shown by the survivors of his "old guard" in a distant state from his home in Alabama, had completely captured him thirty years after taking off his ragged uniform when hostilities closed.

His lovely daughter, Miss Annie, felt proud, indeed, to see the manner in which her noble old father was captured and being compelled to "strike his colors" and surrender for the second time in his life to the force of superior numbers.

MAMMOTH MAGNOLIA TREE 24 FT. IN CIRCUMFERENCE MAGNOLIA PARK

HOUSTON.

FLOW OF ELOQUENCE.

DR. JONES' PRAYER.

N the assembling of the association the first day, Dr. J. William Jones, chaplain, delivered the following invocation:

Oh, God! Our God, our help in years gone by, our hope for years to come—God of Abraham, Isaac and Jacob, God of Israel, God of the centuries, God of our fathers, God of Jefferson Davis, Robert Edward Lee, and Stonewall Jackson, Lord of hosts and King of kings—we bring thee glad and grateful hearts as we gather to-day in our reunion.

We thank thee that, in the world's history, when men have been needed, thou hast raised them up.

We thank thee especially that, in the brave old days of '61-'65, thou didst give to our Southland men—great men—as our leaders, and patriotic heroes of the rank and file, who, often, with bare and bleeding feet, followed their great leaders to an immortality of fame.

We thank thee that, while so many fell in battle, and so many have been falling out of ranks as the years have gone by, yet so many are still spared and so many are permitted to gather in this annual reunion.

God bless every section of our common country—the rulers of the whole land, and of each one of the states, and our whole people. Send us, we beseech thee, fruitful seasons, abundant harvests and returning prosperity, and grant that real peace and plenty may smile upon the land once more. Meet with us, we beseech thee, in this convention; guide, direct and bless us, and send out influence that shall bless the land.

We invoke thy special blessing upon our maimed and needy comrades; that friends may be raised up to supply their wants, and that heaven's richest favor may rest upon them.

Hear us, O God! Answer and bless us, pardon, sanctify and save us, we humbly ask in the name and for the sake of Christ, our dear Redeemer. Amen.

GOVERNOR CULBERSON'S SPEECH.

Hon. Charles A. Culberson, governor of Texas, welcomed the veterans to Texas, as follows:

The American colonists, fleeing from multiplied wrongs of monarchy, established themselves along the Atlantic coast and early became the dominant forces of the continent. They planted there the seed of that revolutionary political faith which developed into our remarkable form of government. The original and commanding proportions of that splendid structure are the marvel of mankind, and its corner-stone, laid thus in a wilderness, and since encircling the earth with its influence, is the fundamental principle of local self-government. Deep-rooted in the affections of the people and essential to the creation and enjoyment of liberty in a representative democracy, its enemies determined that this characteristic of American institutions should neither grow nor be extended. In resistance to British assaults upon it, Jefferson sounded the noblest call to arms since the birth of freedom, and, amid the clash of embattled armies, the foundation of its perpetuity was laid in our organic charter. Nor was the march of the cardinal principle of the revolution wholly arrested elsewhere. Battling for it, rare and noble spirits won imperishable renown in Poland. France, in a revolution dishonored by many cruelties, but founded in just cause, discrowned her king and rebuked the despotism of centuries. Across the English channel that lofty sentiment was maturing for which Emmet offered up his young life, ennobling that heroic and unended struggle for liberty which has been alike the affliction and the glory of his countrymen.

With the victories of Washington and in association with this growth of constitutional government, by common consent of American civilization, grew the unhappy domestic institution of African slavery. In its incipiency and for years afterward it was shared and defended by all. Whatever may have been their motives, whether friendship for the institution or an overshadowing purpose to establish the Union, a majority of Northern with a minority of Southern states engrafted upon the national constitution a recognition of slavery and provided adequate safeguards for its protection. Recognized and guarded by fundamental law, entrenched behind the doctrine of local self-government and wrought into the very tissues of Southern civilization, it may be that its early extinction lay only in revolution; yet, with the lapse of time, its evils were observed by the humanity and statesmanship of all sections. Jefferson hesitated not to denounce it, but compared the solution of the problem to the fearful alternative of holding or unloosing a ferocious beast. Under these surroundings the system continued to be encouraged and extended. With superior marine equipments and trading talents, the North assiduously prosecuted the slave trade until the native increase of the slave population in the South rendered it unprofitable. The inauguration and growth of manufactures in the North, demanding skilled white labor, more favorable climatic conditions and greater demand for slave labor, gradually concentrated the slaves in the South, and they were woven imperceptibly and inexorably into the warp and woof of its social and industrial life. Freed from the conservative and steadying influence of pecuniary interest by the sale of its slaves, the North exhibited an awakened and quickened conscience as to the moral enormity of slavery, and, with increasing bitterness sought its destruction. It was characterized as moral leprosy and its abolition demanded; the constitution of the fathers, because it recognized and protected it, was denounced and execrated and its provisions evaded or openly disregarded; fanatical invasions of states to excite slave insurrection were abetted and applauded; the organic principle of local self-government for the states was denied; the share of the South in the statesmanship and martial glory of the revolution was derided, and Southern character and manners held up to ridicule; and when union ceased to be tolerable upon the theory of affection and consent of the governed, invading armies were mobilized to coerce original and independent sovereignties which had proclaimed that philosophy of govern-

GOVERNOR CULBERSON.

ment and made it immortal. In contradistinction to this, the South in the great controversy stood upon the single and broad contention that the national constitution should be preserved and that the states should be left in their own way and in their own time to solve other than federal problems. This brief and general statement of historic truths is not made in a spirit of offense or crimination. As part of the continuing argument to posterity they are dispassionately recalled as evidence of the provocation and justice of your course, for, while willingly ascribing to Northern soldiers equal integrity of purpose, neither lack of enthusiasm nor political cowardice should deter one of Southern lineage from declaring that for participation in that titanic struggle no apologies need be made to this or future generations. Thus challenged to the arbitrament of the sword, no answer but acceptance could be made. The author of the declaration of independence, the founder of liberty on this continent, the victor in the battles of the revolution, the framer of the constitution of the national republic, and the foremost champion of the reserved rights of the states, the South could not forget the past nor submit to the destruction of its constitutional guarantees and hostile invasion of its territory. The progress and result of the mighty contest which ensued are known of all men. Remembering the masterful and intrepid attack, whether considered with reference to resolute grasp of great questions by the civil administration, under the leadership of that illustrious man whose daughters honor us with their presence, or the brilliant operations of the land and naval forces, the defense of the South in vigor and heroism is without a parallel. Out of scant material and resources a strong and powerful government was constructed and to the end was administered by statesmen worthy the gigantic struggle in which they were engaged. Less than a dozen warships, commanded by the equals of Decatur and Nelson, successfully patrolled and expelled the Union merchant marine from American waters. In military conceptions as bold and comprehensive as those of Napoleon or Wellington, and in charges more brilliant than those of Murat or Cardigan, the armies astonished and electrified the world. Every land was dazzled with their deeds and the universe emblazoned with their glory. Brave as Spartans and knightly as the old cavaliers, "somewhere in eternity within some golden palace walls where old imperial banners float and Launcelots keep guard and Arthurs reign and all the patriot heroes dwell," they will abide with brothers.

Now that the passions of the great civil strife sleep in patriotic oblivion and only its loftier impulses are treasured, it is appropriate that the survivors of the Confederacy should meet in fraternal reunion. This great state is honored by your coming and it is the proudest of my official acts in her name to welcome you cordially to her soil and the hospitalities of her people. It is fitting that the brave should meet here, in a noble city named for Houston, within cannon-sound of the battle field of San Jacinto, in a state that has measured glory with the ancients, and upon whose every hearthstone the fires of patriotism still burn. Crowned with the glories of battle and decked with the flowers of peace,

> " When the golden sunset
> Fades into the distant west,
> Rays of its parting splendor
> Fall on your place of rest ;
> Then to the silent churchyard
> Love's footsteps shall fondly stray
> To pray for the souls of heroes
> Who fought for the south and the gray."

JUDGE JAMES MASTERSON'S RESIDENCE,
THE HOME OF MISS WINNIE DAVIS WHILE IN HOUSTON.

GENERAL GORDON'S SPEECH.

General John B. Gordon, commander-in-chief of the United Confederate Veterans' Association, responded to the welcoming addresses as follows:

Governor, Mr. Mayor, Comrades and Fellow-Citizens—It is my official duty and high privilege to respond in behalf of my comrades to this gracious welcome and tender of munificent hospitality by the city of Houston and state of Texas. When I have said that they are characteristic of this city and state, my language is capable of no stronger expression. What higher tribute could be paid to this great people than to say that their hospitality is worthy of Texas? Around the name and history of Texas are gathered associations glorious and hallowed; and in her future career are centered high hopes of richest contribution to the republic.

In fifty years of statehood she has risen to a commanding position among her sisters; and the imagination can scarcely keep pace with her assured progress in the fifty years to come. With a genial climate and imperial domain, with a soil not only exhaustless in its fertility, but which, like responsive charity, answers with more lavish abundance as the demands upon it become more exacting; with a history rich in the memories of her Alamo, her Goliad, her San Jacinto, as well as the deeds of her Houston, her Austin, her Travis and her Lamar; with a proud heritage of valor and heroism, bequeathed by her intrepid sons in the mighty conflict of the sixties; with some of the best blood of the republic in the veins of her people, whose indomitable energy and lofty spirit are equaled only by their princely hospitality; with all these splendid endowments by nature, by history, and by the characteristics of her sons and her daughters, what optimistic prophet could predict for her a career so glorious as to be beyond her reasonable ambition?

The assembling of the war-scarred veterans in this war-scarred state recalls a striking contrast in the war history. Sixty years ago Texas won her fight for independence. Thirty years ago these ex-Confederates lost their fight for separate nationality; but Texas, victorious, was no more glorious and grand than were these brave men around me in their overwhelming defeat.

Texas, victorious, won her way to statehood and a place in the front ranks of states. The Confederates, crushed and disbanded as soldiers, addressed themselves to the duties of citizens with a conservatism so conspicuous, a patriotism so true and broad, a fidelity to the decisions of battles unquestioned and sincere, as to challenge the confidence and esteem of patriots in every section of the Union.

This leads me to recall three remarkable achievements by these ex-Confederates in peace which impartial history will pronounce a fitting climax to their splendid record in war. The first is the reconstruction, mainly through your instrumentality, of the labor system of the entire section. You returned from a long, exhausting and unsuccessful struggle to find the agricultural labor of your states not only disorganized, but as a system (to the management and control of which you were born and trained), it was utterly destroyed. Yet you heroically undertook the task of its reorganization under a new system, and, adapting yourselves to that new order, the success of your efforts is the noblest commentary upon your wisdom and justice. With no power to control that hitherto servile labor, with no money to pay it, you successfully guided it to a

HOUSTON HOMES.

plane of self-support and to vastly increased production of the South's great staple.

The second is your astounding success in securing, in spite of the radical revolution in the conditions around you, and in so short a period, financial independence for your families and industrial prosperity for your section. You returned from the war poor, the first of thousands penniless, many shot and maimed, and yet bravely and uncomplainingly laboring with aid from no source save from God and your own self-reliance and manhood. You have fought your way to competence, provided for our disabled comrades until scarcely a Confederate soldier can be found deprived of the comforts of life. At the same time your combined efforts have carried these Southern states to a height of material advancement from which you may now calmly look back over a land which but thirty years ago was a wide waste of desolation and ashes, and around you over a country now happy in its rebuilt homes and redeemed farms, radiant in the light of industrial resurrection, of assured prosperity and enduring material independence.

The third achievement is the passionless, unostentatious and peaceful manner in which you laid aside the trappings and discipline of the camp for the garb of the citizen and silent restraints of civil government. For this marvelous exhibition of self-command under supremest trials; for this complete burial of all sectional bitterness; for the gradual but certain transmuting of your valor and devotion, exhibited in defense of the dead that fell into unchallenged loyalty to the flag that triumphed—to all these evidences of the loftiest attributes of citizenship, you will find your reward in the universal plaudits of your countrymen as it is already secured in the power, progress and cherished freedom of our reunited republic.

Go forward, my comrades, and by self-denial, by wise economy and well-directed energy, continue the material development of this heaven-blessed section until abundance shall be found in every home, and the whole land shall rejoice in your industrial triumph. Go forward in the cultivation of a national fraternity, giving no heed to imprudent or thoughtless efforts to stimulate sectional animosities in any quarter.

I rejoice in the privilege of bearing to you fraternal greetings from the great body of men who confronted you in battle. It has been my fortune recently to mingle with those men in every section. Be assured, my Confederate comrades, that the overwhelming majority of the Grand Army of the Republic, composed of soldiers who were brave in battle and are generous in peace, courageous, knightly and true, bear toward you neither lingering bitterness nor sentiment of distrust. Whatever of untimely passion may here exist from any cause will be of short duration and comparatively harmless. In the presence of your continued conservatism, and in view of the higher and nobler sentiment of the country, it will vanish as the vapors before the morning sun.

But I must not consume more of the time of this most important convention. I close as I began, by assuring the governor of this great state, the mayor of this metropolitan city, and the generous and patriotic people of both, that the United Confederate Veterans are profoundly grateful for this superb reception and bountiful hospitality.

HOUSTON HOMES.

SPEECH OF DR. J. WILLIAM JONES.

WHEN the report of the Davis monument committee was under consideration, Chaplain J. William Jones, of Virginia, spoke as follows:

Mr. President—I second the motion to adopt this report, and heartily endorse the appeal of my gallant old friend, General Cabell.

So far as Jefferson Davis is concerned, he needs no monument. The man who, as soldier, illustrated bright pages of American history, and saved the day at Buena Vista by his cool bravery and marvelous skill—who, as statesman, graced the senate of the United States when there "were giants in the land," and was the peer of the "great triumvirate"—Clay, Calhoun and Webster—who was a peerless orator—who was the greatest secretary of war the country ever had, and left many improvements which are now blessing the service; who was a patriot true and tried, and who was a high-toned, Christian gentleman, without fear and without reproach—this man has, indeed, "erected a monument more lasting than bronze," and needs no granite or marble to perpetuate his memory.

He is no longer "the uncrowned king of his people," but they have crowned him with loving hearts, and he lives forever in their affections.

But we owe it to ourselves, and to the great principles of constitutional freedom, for which we fought, and of which Jefferson Davis was the embodiment that we should rear this monument to teach our children that we were true to duty in the day of trial.

I know not why it is that our president has had heaped upon him the bitterest abuse and most malignant slanders of our enemies—that he seems to have been singled out for their especial hatred. I heard General Lee say once: "I do not know why they should be so bitter against Mr. Davis. He only did what he could to establish the independence of the South, and the rest of us tried to do the same. If he is guilty of any crime, the rest of us are equally guilty."

We owe it to ourselves and to posterity that we should build this monument in the old capital of the Confederacy, and let it proclaim to future generations that our beloved chief was no "rebel" and no "traitor," but as pure a patriot as the world ever saw.

Now, I know that I am sometimes called "an reconstructed rebel," but I emphatically deny that either you or I were ever "rebels" at all.

George Washington and his compatriots were "rebels" because they fought against properly constituted authority, but we were not "rebels," because we fought to uphold the constitution of our fathers.

NO REBELS IN THE SOUTH.

If there were any rebels in that war they did not live in the South, but north of the Potomac and the Ohio. They were the men who denounced the constitution of our fathers as "a league with death and a covenant with hell," and who fought to overthrow the great principles of constitutional freedom, for which Jefferson Davis and Robert Lee drew their stainless swords.

And since we furled our glorious battle flags, parked our blackened guns (nearly all of them wrested from the enemy in battle), stacked our bright muskets and gave our paroles, there have been no more law-abiding, peacable, better citizens of the states and of the United States on this continent than these old Confederate soldiers.

Our honored commander—the gallant, chivalric Gordon, one of Lee's trusted Paladins—but voiced the sentiment of the people of our Southland when he stood up on the floor of the senate and pledged us to stand by the government in suppressing rebellion at Chicago.

And when our "lame lion," the peerless orator, Senator John W. Daniel,

J. WILLIAM JONES.

of Virginia, offered his resolutions endorsing the president in enforcing the law, he but echoed the sentiments of his Confederate comrades.

Yes, we are all loyal citizens of these United States, ready to unite with our brethren of every section to make our common country the grandest, the freest, the most prosperous that the sun shines upon. "Old Glory!" Why should we not march under its folds and glory in its lustre? It was designed from the coat of arms of our Washington. "The Star-Spangled Banner was written by a Southern man, when Southern troops had just won a glorious victory on Southern soil. Our Taylor, our Scott, our Jefferson Davis, our J. E. Johnston, our Robert Edward Lee, our Magruder, our Albert Sidney Johnston, our Stonewall Jackson, our Beauregard, and others of that brilliant galaxy of Southern officers bore it on the most glorious fields of Mexico and planted it on the walls of the Montezumas.

It is true that we fought against it for four years, when it represented what was abhorrent to our views of constitutional freedom, but it is our flag still, and we can join with heart and soul in singing:

> " The Star-Spangled Banner,
> Oh, long may it wave
> O'er the land of the free
> And the home of the brave."

But while this is true let it be distinctly understood that we are not going around with our fingers in our mouths, whimpering and whining and asking pardon and promising to do so no more. But with head erect we look the world squarely in the eyes and say: "We thought we were right in the brave old days, when to do battle was sacred duty, but now, in the light of subsequent events, we know we were right," and with malice for none and charity for all, we are asking pardon of no living man.

We are not ashamed of the cause for which we fought; of the men who led us, or of the fight we made against "overwhelming numbers and resources." Let us embody these sentiments in a noble monument to our grand old president.

We have already in the capital of our confederacy monuments to our Christian soldiers, Stonewall Jackson, and gallant A. P. Hill, and peerless Robert Lee, and the true hero of the war, the private soldier of the Confederacy. Let us now cap it all with this monument, and make it worthy of Jefferson Davis and the cause he loved so well.

That noble report on history presented on yesterday by that gallant, glorious soldier and stainless gentleman, Stephen D. Lee, embodies principles that we ought to carry home with us and put in practice until every Northern school history is banished from our schools, and every book slandering our Confederate people, our leaders, and our cause, is banished from our libraries and our homes. Let us also utilize the enthusiasm of this hour and put in granite and bronze the life-speaking embodiment of these principles. I have traveled 1428 miles to come here, and I would readily travel 14,000 miles to witness the scene here on yesterday, when we hailed and greeted the "daughter of the Confederacy," and she acknowledged it with that queenly grace which made us crown her queen of our hearts. God bless her.

But I shall count it a higher privilege still if I may carry back home the assurance that the veterans of our Southland will unite, hearts and hands, in honoring themselves by rearing this monument.

It has been already delayed too long. Let us now make a united effort that shall accomplish it in the near future. Many camps and communities propose collections for this object on the approaching 3d of June, the anniversary of the birth of Jefferson Davis.

This is appropriate and well, and I urge that this plan be generally carried out.

But there ought to be some expression here and now of our purpose to raise this fund at once.

I knew some years ago an old deacon who got his church out of many a financial strait by the stereotyped speech: "Well, brethren, the way to do a thing is to do it. I will give ten dollars. How much will you give, Brother Smith?"

Let us now call the roll of our camps, and have responses worthy of the cause and of ourselves.

JEFFERSON DAVIS IN 1866.

Dr. Jones then engineered a subscription that ran up to over ten thousand dollars, and it was confidently believed that, had there been time, this sum would have been more than doubled, and that the enthusiasm engendered will result in a very large increase of the fund.

GENERAL WISE'S SPEECH.

When nominations for the place of the next meeting were declared in order, General Peyton F. Wise, of Virginia, ascended the platform and delivered the following splendid oration:

After a weary journey of 1400 miles, I rejoice to be at last upon the soil of Texas. I rejoice that although I am here for the first time, and at the end of so long an interval from my mother state, I am yet as much at home here as there. I rejoice most of all that I am a veteran among veterans of the best army that ever trod the earth. My wife, who is a veteran, too, in every fiber of her, except her years, put my badge on and smoothed the wrinkles out of my Lee camp uniform and bade me come hither upon the plea that these encampments must, in a sense, soon cease, and that the number of those who attend them must be fewer and fewer as the years roll by, until they all become a tale that has been told. Not so, I told her, with a little tear over the constancy, the fortitude, the devotion, the pluck of the women. I stand here to-day in the midst of ranks that never were or will be broken by the loss of a single soldier, true to his cause and his home. All the clods of all the valleys, with all their rest-breathing daisies, nay, Ossa piled upon Peleon of superincumbent burial, could never keep away from his roll-call and his bivouac a single brave heart that ever stood for honor upon the field of honor. Lee and Jackson, the Johnstons and Hood, Stuart and Forrest, are just as real as the splendid soldier who wields yonder baton to-day. The choir that raised the rebel yell never lost a note. All its music in highest register goes sounding down the ages because it is the paean of glory. The Confederate flag was never folded, was never weary, although the patriot Ryan told us so, because it was always symbolled and will always symbol immortal liberties whose fitting home is its stars. It will float forever upon every heaven-kissing breeze.

I am at home here, because I am the brother of every man who went to immortal glory at the bidding of him who once led Hood's fighting brigade; of every man, of all those who offered the Sterling Price of unwearying constancy and devotion for the safety and honor of the common heritage; of every bishop who doffed the priestly garment and rallied around him the Creole and the Anglo-Saxon, the children of the civil and the common law alike, to be in serried ranks in the very van of liberty; of every Mississippian who followed the lead of that Lee who, in war emulated the highest glories of a name which seems to have always been associated with what is best and truest in arms, and who survived in peace to illustrate that the gentleness of woman is always the associate of the bravest heart; of every man who never became restless in the doing of his heart-work, if only because fighting Joe Wheeler was in the lead and would never stay while the soil of his country was encumbered by a foe; of every man who ever dozed under a palmetto tree, to be more alert when Hampton rescued from the red field of carnage the white plume of Stuart and kept it always stainless in his heart and upon his head; of every man of the land of Macon who found a new inspiration in the name of one of the "noblest Romans of them all"—

SCENES ON =:
BUFFALO BAYOU..........

HOUSTON.

that D. H. Hill, upon whose countenance dwelt in comeliest fashion the light and smile of battle, because the Tar Heel pathway was the road to duty; of every countryman of him who made Shiloh a tale to be told forever because the ablest tactician, the most princely form, sat upon his horse, in the very forefront of the fight, calmly sat with a smile upon his face, dealing triumph to his men till the last refluence of his heart's blood surged upon his spurs, whose watch, wherever it may be to-day, whether in worthy or unworthy hands, will tell the time of day only to the highest manhood, the most Christian knight; of every follower of him who was and is the hero of the common people, the example of the fact that in the Forrests as in courts are to be found the Napoleons with a star, and finally of every comrade of to-day who hangs upon the lips of him who was the bow of promise to every man in the Southern army who feared that danger might come too close to Lee, and who has lived to show how a man surcharged with the most loving memories of a past that was filled with the glories and liberties of his section, may be the most orderly, the most faithful, the most devoted servant of the whole country. God bless Gordon and keep his scarred face long as the seal of a holy consecration.

And, finally, you are my brothers, and Virginia is your own, who ever saw the gleam of the best and bluest and truest saber that ever flashed athwart the sky of war, who fattened her soil with your blood and made her illustrious forever by your immortal valor. Amen, and Amen!

I come to invite you to make your next encampment in my city; to sound the bugle call of another and a different "On to Richmond;" to those who have a right to be there, with or without invitation, because they shed their blood to save, not to win her. Her official bodies, her council and her chamber of commerce greet you thro' us and bid you come and stand upon her hills, and by her flowing river; to see how the city of your love, which is your very own, the chosen seat of your Confederacy, has fared as a trust in their hands; how they have built her up in forms of beauty and things of life to be worthy of your renewed adoption. Her women, not less true because some men have been, fainthearted, fallen by the wayside and no longer care for the goal, not less sweet because they no longer feed upon the sorghum of those times, not less gorgeously appareled because they no longer attire themselves in the homespun and the makeshifts of the good old days, but always wearing the true colors and their hearts upon their sleeves, whether balloon or skin tight, ask you with all their might and main and with all their dear hearts to come. Fifty thousand of your dead, who sleep in Hollywood and Oakwood, who are the children of every state in the Confederacy, ask to have you commune with them to catch the inspiration, which will make the New South, it may be in fairer flowers in more fields, in fatter cattle upon larger hills, in busier hum of more varied industries, but continue the Old South always in all that tends to the high manhood and makes, to the real glory.

The very stones of her streets cry aloud to be trodden again by those who traversed them on their way to her battle fronts—to every field where charged to victory the army of Northern Virginia, and where swelled upon the air the chorus of the rebel yell.

Her monuments majectically summon you to come. In her eastern section, upon the hill of the church, where broke from Henry's frenzied lips the crip of "Liberty or death," stands in human form the echo of that cry—the private soldier of the Confederate states, the soldier that, multiplied, whether hungry and tentless or fed and sheltered, whether travel-stained and weary or fresh

THE HOUSTON LIGHT GUARDS.

COMPANY AND ARMORY.

from slumber upon the bosom of his mother earth, made the best army that the world ever knew. The earth cannot contain his glory, because it ascends to heaven, and because he is unique—the one soldier that earth ever produced who was general as well as soldier. He stands, they say, upon Pompey's Pillar. Not so. He was no selfish conqueror. His lofty column is his own; standing upon his own soil, made of stones dug from the bowels of his own hills, and fashioned by his own people. The rags, thank God, have droped from his limbs. He is as jaunty and trim as the smartest blue coat of them all. The lean and hungry look has fled from his face. The inspired artist has obeyed Christ's injunction to "feed His lambs." His back is to the Chickahominy because the enemy is no longer there; his face is turned toward his city, because he wants to watch the business of his people, and watch to see if it be fairly and squarely done. His musket is not as bright as of yore. It has been bronzed to keep it always ready to be the impregnable defense of the liberties of his people.

Here in the central station, in the chief seat, is the best piece of monumental art in all the world. Its crowning feature is he, who, surrounded by the best statesmen of the revolutionary era, and although sitting upon a war horse that sniffeth the battle from afar, is yet majestic and dignified, himself pointing the ways of peace and war and above all that freedom is the surest foundation of progress and happiness. Aye, he is the father of his country. Hardby, the gift of the mother of the Anglo-Saxon people to the best representatives of the Anglo-Saxon race that ever trod this globe, stands he of the Cromwell mold, he, the Old Testament Christian, the sword of the Lord and of Gideon upon him, ready as ever to smite hip and thigh; and he shall stand there forever, a Stonewall to memorialize the way in which Virginia and her sisters should be defended.

There, upon a splendid boulevard more beautiful than the elysian fields which lead to Napoleon's Arch of Triumph, or than the linden which shade the statue of Frederick the Great, stands a martial figure, ever alert to catch the last order of Jackson which rang out like a clarion just before he crossed over the river to rest under the shade trees—"Let A. P. Hill prepare for action."

Yonder in the West, in the region of the setting sun, with magnificent poise of figure and face as of soul, fit as always to lead the hosts of the earth, rides Lee, riding towards the jocund day that stands tiptoe upon the peak of paradise, when he shall be fitter still, fit to marshal the very hosts of heaven.

Anon will rise the simulacrum of the bold and fearless rider, the fiercest paladin, and the gentlest gentleman, the man with the nerve of the whirlwind, whether he kept a dainty slipper from the mud or held the common weal of a nation upon the couch of his lance, the smile of utmost joy on his face, whether he listened to the strains of Swinny's banjo or charged better than the Six Hundred at Balaklava, the very presentiment, let it be, of our own darling Jeb Stuart.

But there is a monument which shall be, but which God save the mark, is yet unbuilded, which most of all, orders you to come. Did I say yet to be builded? Again, I say, God save the mark. By the riverside of Hendrick Hudson's flowing river, just away from the busiest hum of the most multitudinous city, just on the skirts of a progress seemingly the most splendid because it is the most selfish, rises apace an erection, the free gift, without gleaning from the public stare, of a free people, lifted above their progress, stealing away from their hum, to be grateful to the savior of the people's Union. An illustrious soldier and president is to be canonized in the affections of a people every way composite, and the expression of that affection is to be a heaven-kissing monument. Let Grant's monument rise, the higher the better, the sooner the more fitting. He

OFFICERS OF THE HOUSTON LIGHT GUARD.

deserved it. He was not composite; he was genuine, unadulterated, unlimited Saxon pluck and pertinacity, fighting always in the splendid way in which God gave him to fight for the thing he believed in and loved. He deserved it, even from us, if only because in the moment of his triumph he mounted no triumphal car but said, "Let us have peace," and acted it. But for him and dead Lincoln, what would have become of the Union, even after the war?

But shall his monument arise quicker than our monument, the monument of us, the homogenous, us. the best expression of the all-subduing, the Anglo-Saxon race; us, the most capable, because the most inspired; us, the most obligated, because the most blessed; us, who love our public men, because we make them and they are part of us; us, who are inspired by their examples, because like the south wind upon a bank of violets, which steals and gives their odor, we teach them what to inspire.

What, then, is our monument, and by the name of what one of us shall it be called, although it be the monument of every one of us? It shall be a monument to Jefferson Davis, president of the Confederate states of America, in the capital of the Confederate states of America; and the prime duty of this grand encampment in the spring of 1896, when men's hearts are budding like the flowers and turning to love, to lay its corner-stone in Richmond. Who, then, was Jefferson Davis? Born in the north of us in the land which Virginia gave to the United States, he lived in the south of us. He knew us, on every side of us, in every part of us. Inspiring and inspired by us, impregnated by us and filling us in turn, he became the very type and father of us. He had known every joy which can fill the human heart. Blessed is his store, thrice blessed is his home; he led that happiest of all lives, the life of a cultured country gentleman. First found in public he was leading his Mississippians to immortal fame upon the plains of Buena Vista. He became in turn representative, senator, cabinet officer, president, his name blown about the world as the leader of established order, of a new essay of the Anglo-Saxon race, in freer government, as the commander in chief of an army the like of which for valor and fortitude the world had never seen. By and by the shadows came. At the very pinnacle of his freedom, the gyves were put upon his wrists. At the moment when, at Fortress Monroe, he had learned to mount with the eagle and to look with eagle's eyes upon the sun, the sun went down and a bull's-eye lantern scorched his very eyeballs. In the very nick of his truth to his people, to liberty and to law, he was dubbed a traitor and commended to brand and penalty as a felon.. He was the vicar of your manacles, of your tortured eyesight, of your imputed treason and felony. He bore his suffering with all the pluck of Confederate armies, with all the grace and sweetness and dignity of Lee. He was worthy of you. But there were righteous judges in those days, the charges slunk away, ashamed to pollute his presence, and his suffering ended. Once more he is the inmate of a country home, once more blessed by the woman who exalts and who consoles, in the person of his noble wife, in the person of his noble daughter, who has become the daughter of every one of us because she was born in our Confederacy and because she was his daughter, and because she is one of the noblest of all noble women. There he lived until he was gathered to our other dead, and was brought to be buried on the banks of that river which brought the first of the Saxons to our shore, and murmurs its sweet requiem to one of the best and last of them. It is his monument that is our monument, whose corner-stone you shall lay in 1896. Will you, can you, refuse? I think not.

INCIDENTS OF SPECIAL INTEREST.

RECEPTION AT LIGHT GUARD ARMORY.

Miss Winnie Davis attended a reception at the armory of the famous Houston Light Guard, on Wednesday evening, given in her honor. Thousands of people gathered in and about the great building, eager to grasp the hand of the daughter of the Confederacy—thousands more than could get inside the hall. It was calculated that at one time five thousand people were gathered upon the streets outside. Seeing the disappointment pictured upon their faces, Colonel Lombard, of New Orleans, a friend of Miss Davis, conducted her to the balcony, where she could at least be seen by the multitude below. The cheering with which they greeted her appearance showed the reverent love held by the people of the South for the daughter of the man who suffered all for their sake and the sake of principle. After seeing Miss Davis, the outside crowd quickly and quietly dispersed.

A wonderfully touching incident occurred during this reception. A short, sparely built old gentleman, with hair and beard of snowy whiteness, approached Miss Davis and, taking her by the hand, said: "My child, it was these arms that carried you into the prison at Fortress Monroe to visit your father when he was imprisoned there. Ah, how tenderly he took you from me, and how lovingly he kissed and fondled you. And when you had stayed with him the allotted time, I bore you back again to your mother."

Throwing her arms about the old veteran's neck, the "baby girl" of the South's great chieftain sobbed upon his shoulder, while down his cheeks, which the finger of time has failed to wrinkle, the flowing tears couresd from eyes unused to weep.

The little old gentleman was ex-Governor Frank R. Lubbock, of Texas, who was with President Davis at his capture and during his confinement.

W. A. CHILDRESS,
MANAGER U. C. V. REUNION ASSOCIATION,
HOUSTON.

W. D. CLEVELAND,
PRESIDENT U. C. V. REUNION ASSOCIATION,
HOUSTON.

JOHN T. BROWNE,
MAYOR OF HOUSTON.

BY THE WAYSIDE.

HERE never was anything like it, is what everybody says. There never was such bunting, there never were such banners and decorations, and so many things to stir the heart and dim the eye! The windows are filled with objects of interest, many of them beautiful, and many more filled with pathos. Here was a stained and tattered banner, the legend beneath it telling in what bloody battle it was borne and where shot and shell tore through it; and the old soldiers gather about and gaze at it with mournful interest, and tell one another, "I was there—marched behind that old flag!" There was a sword, rusting in its scabbard now for many a day, while the hands that drew it once are folded away in their last repose. Here was an old-fashioned spinning wheel, with the rolls and cards at hand, and the woman knitting an old-fashioned sock of coarse, homemade thread, in quite the old-fashioned way; and there in another window were the old cannon balls and rusty shot and shell that were the ghastly trophies of old battle fields. Flags, guns, worn-out gray suits—what histories are connected with them all! No wonder the throngs of visitors pass by the elegant displays of goods to gaze upon these patriotic mementoes of the struggle that took so much out of their lives!

The most pathetic feature of the reunion is the tender feeling the veterans entertain for the daughter of their old leader. No woman in the history of the world was ever given such homage; was ever adopted into the inmost hearts of an entire people and looked upon as the beloved child of the country. It was touching beyond description to see the gray-haired veterans struggling to get near enough to pat her hand, and weep-

CAMP WINNIE DAVIS, WAXAHATCHIE, TEXAS, U. C. V.

This camp attended the reunion one hundred and eight strong, in a beautifully decorated chair car, upon the sides of which were striking likenesses in color of Generals Joe Johnston, Beauregard, Jackson and Gordon, and battle flags with the names of all battles in which the members participated. The car decorations, which "surpassed all others at Houston," were by Professor Cohen.

ing as they touched it. The American people are supposed to be incapable of hero worship, and to hold no one sacred from criticism; yet this one woman is the idol of a people, worshiped with a chivalrous devotion. "Hurrah for our Winnie!" cried one of the graybeards, waving his hat in air; and by his side another shouted, "God bless our little girl!" Down the steps of the armory came two old men, rough and poor and hard-handed, but the tears were shining on their homely faces and giving them a kind of glory in spite of their homeliness. "Did you see her?" asked one of them with a shaken voice; and the other cried, "Yes, I did, and shook her pretty little hand, God bless her!" Even the old negro who managed to reach her and to shake that ready and gracious hand, cried with a smile that shone through tears, "God bless you, Miss Winnie, I come from ole Mississippi, an' I've been on your pa's place many a time." No woman has been so honored—few women ought to be so happy.

A BEAUTIFUL TRIBUTE.

There was a scene enacted at the reception of Miss Winnie Davis at the Capitol Hotel on Thursday which brought tears to the eyes of many who witnessed it. Judge Norman G. Kittrell had escorted his mother and her grandmother (the latter Mrs. Sarah W. Goree, who is in her eighty-ninth year and who had traveled more than one hundred miles to attend the reunion, thirty miles of the distance by private conveyance). Mrs. Goree had five sons in the Confederate army, three in Hood's brigade, all of whom came back wounded, while her eldest, Major Thomas J. Goree, was on Longstreet's staff from Bull Run to Appomattox, and the fifth served in the trans-Mississippi department. Three of her sons were here to meet her. She was most graciously received by Mrs. Rice, and her clear black eyes and placid but intelligent face, set in a lace cap, the white ribbons of which fell over her black satin dress of becoming pattern, made a picture that attracted instant attention, and she held a levee second only in proportion to that of Miss Davis herself.

When Mrs. Goree was presented to Mrs. J. C. Hutcheson the latter at once led her forward and presented her to Miss Davis, who received her with the utmost grace and cordiality. Turning for the while from the hundreds thronging around her, she bent low and held the hand of the venerable lady in both her own, and assured her again and again of the pleasure she felt in meeting her. When the last pressure was given Mrs. Goree raised the hand of Miss Davis to her lips and kissed it. Whereupon Miss Davis said: "Oh, no; it is not for you to kiss my hand, but for me to kiss yours," and still holding the thin hand of the grandmother in hers she knelt to the floor and kissed it tenderly and with a caress well nigh holy—thus paying the tribute of a noble woman to the mother of five Confederate soldiers. Such a scene is worthy of the poet's pen and the artist's brush. Many an eye moistened as the scene was so touchingly enacted.

GENERAL WILLIAM P. HARDEMAN.
"OLD GOTCH."

CANE PRESENTATION.

The parlor of the Hutchins House was the scene of an affecting incident. Green's Brigade Association, just at adjournment, decided to present General W. P. Hardeman a cane. Miss Lydia Kirk, "the daughter of the brigade," was selected to make the presentation. Miss Lydia played her part well, until her feelings overcame her, when she threw her arms around the old man's neck, kissed him and melted down in tears. The general, "Old Gotch," as the boys call him, gave way to his feelings, crying like a child; and, to make the tableaux complete, all the grizzly old "Confeds"—a parlor full of them—surrounded "Old Gotch" and Miss Lydia. As one of them expressed it, "Did you ever see such a gang of blubbering old fools as we are?"

THOMAS M. MURFREE.

Thomas M. Murfree, of Troy, Alabama, was the most conspicuous as a veteran private at Houston. He moved about with an elastic, boyish step in the Confederate gray coat that appears in his picture. He is a native Tennesseean, but his family moved to Alabama in 1845, when he was two years old.

Murfree enlisted in the Independent Rifles in 1861, which was a part of the Sixth Alabama Regiment, to the command of which General John B. Gordon was elected in the reorganization at Yorktown, Virginia. Comrade Murfree was not absent from his command, except on detached duty, until his transfer to the Tennessee army in 1863.

This is the identical coat that Murfree took from his body to pillow General Gordon's head when so severely wounded at Sharpsburg. It was at that time General Gordon thought he had been killed, and while meditating upon his death, he fancied that if the mind was so clear it might enable him to move the dead foot. Anyhow, he concluded to try it. After the movement of the foot, he realized that he could move his body, and was not dead. Murfree was made lieutenant in Loring's division, and was at Franklin, Nashville and at Bentonville, North Carolina. He was offered one hundred dollars for his old gray coat.

DR. HYAM COHEN WITH FLAG OF CAMP WINNIE DAVIS.

One of the most conspicuous veterans at Houston was Dr. Hyam Cohen, of Waxahatchie, Texas. Although small, he stood erect, under a silk hat that he would not have worn thirty-three years ago, "dressed like a Philadelphia lawyer," and carried, wherever he went, the magnificent flag that he holds in the picture. The very handsome flag presented to the camp by him is forty by fifty-six inches. Upon one side, which is crimson silk, is a splendid painting, which is a finely executed likeness of General Robert E. Lee on "Traveler," sword in hand, eyes flashing fire,

as he rusehd to the front at the "Wilderness." Amid smoke and bursting
shell is the background. In the foreground is a wounded soldier reeling.
dismounted cannon, and other war material. On the reverse side, which is
Confederate blue, are the fine gold letters: "Camp Winnie Davis, Waxahatchie, Texas, U. C. V.. Organized February 10, 1890." The flag has
a deep, gold fringe, and is mounted on an elegant staff eight feet long,
surmounted by a gold spear, from the base of which hang two heavy gold
cords with massive gold tassels. The design, painting and mounting
were made by Professor L. L. Cohen, a brother of Dr. Cohen.

•

N 1894 the citizens of Houston. having determined that the reunion for 1895 should be held
in their city, sent to the reunion at Birmingham,
for the purpose of bringing about that result,
the following committee:

Mayor John T. Browne, chairman; B. R.
Warner, secretary and treasurer; L. T. Noyes,
J. H. Bright, W. H. Crank, Sr., Will Lambert,
Norman G. Kittrell, R. M. Johnston, C. C. Bea-
vens, G. H. Bringhurst, J. R. Waties, S. D.
Moore, Robert Adair, T. U. Lubbock.

Governor J. S. Hogg also attended and was
a guest of the committee, which traveled in a special car, retaining same
for use at Birmingham.

After the committee had returned home, having accomplished its
mission, the citizens set about preparing for the meeting, which they knew
would be the biggest that had ever assembled in Texas. The United Confederate Veterans' Reunion Association was formed with the following
officers: President, W. D. Cleveland; first vice president, John T.
Browne; second vice president, H. W. Garrow; treasurer, T. W. House;
secretary, B. R. Warner.

An executive committee was selected from the association to take
charge of all the details of the reunion, as follows: W. A. Childress, chairman and general manager; B. R. Warner, secretary; R. M. Johnston,
F. A. Reichardt, Spencer Hutchins, H. F. MacGregor, L. T. Noyes, William Christian, J. M. Cotton, H. B. Rice.

Sub-committees were appointed, with chairmen as follows:

Public Comfort—J. R. Waties, chairman.

Amusements—Norman G. Kittrell, chairman.

Decoration—S. R. S. Andres, chairman.

Finance—T. W. House, chairman.

Transportation—Charles B. Peck, chairman, vice C. Lombardi, resigned on account of absence.

Invitation—John T. Browne, chairman.

Building—R. D. Gribble, chairman.

Reception—Dick Dowling Camp; Will Lambert, chairman.

General chairman Ladies' Auxiliary, Mrs. S. W. Sydnor; Miss Mary Root, secretary.

Press Reception—W. W. Dexter, chairman.

Military—H. B. Rice, chairman.

Ex-Federals—A. K. Taylor, chairman.

Grounds—Richard Cocke, chairman.

Ladies' Reception—Mrs. J. C. Hutcheson, chairman.

Ladies' Military Banquet—Mrs. J. F. Dickson, chairman.

Ladies' Press Banquet—Mrs. J. A. Huston, chairman.

Ladies' Decoration—Mrs. L. T. Noyes, chairman.

All these committees labored hard to make the affair a success, many of the most diligent and intelligent workers being those whose names appear upon no official roster.

Two of these unofficial helpers who did valiant service were Mrs. R. Rutherford and Mr. Harvey T. D. Wilson.

Mrs. Rutherford organized and carried out a scheme by which all veterans who so desired would be furnished their meals free while in the city, and many an old soldier was thus hospitably entertained without money and without price.

Mr. Wilson, who is the owner of a beautiful driving park, situated in the suburbs of the city, donated to the association its use as a camp ground during the reunion.

GALVESTON.

No account of the great reunion, however brief, would be adequate that did not include the royal hospitality of Galveston. Round trip excur-

VIEW OF THE JETTIES AT GALVESTON.

sions were given over the fifty miles at one dollar. Camp McGruder, one of the best Confederate organizations, turned out daily to give welcome and possession. Free excursions were given by boat to the jetties several miles out, and to other points, and free chowder, with coffee, etc., was

THE DOCKS IN GALVESTON.

served near one of the pleasant lakes on the island to the multitude.

There was not a veteran there, perhaps, who will fail to recall, in connection with this reunion, in especial gratitude, their fraternity and open-hearted hospitality.

JESSE FRY, JR.

Living Confederate Generals.

HERE were during the war four hundred and ninety-eight generals of the several grades commissioned in the Confederate army. Of this number the following still survive:

Lieutenant Generals.

Stephen D. Lee, Starkville, Miss.; James Longstreet, Gainesville, Ga.; Simon B. Buckner, Frankfort, Ky.; Joseph Wheeler, Wheeler, Ala.; Alexander P. Stewart, Chickamauga, Ga.; Wade Hampton, Columbia, S. C.; John B. Gordon, Atlanta, Ga.

Major Generals.

Gustavus W. Smith, New York; Lafayette McLaws, Savannah, Ga.; Samuel D. French, Winter Park, Ala.; John H. Forney, Jenifer, Ala.; Dabney H. Maury, Richmond, Va.; Henry Heth, Antietam battle field survey; J. L. Kemper, Orange Court House, Va.; Robert F. Hoke, Raleigh, N. C.; Fitzhugh Lee, Glasgow, Va.; W. B. Bate, United States senate, Tennessee; M. C. Butler, United States senate, South Carolina; E. C. Walthall, United States senate Mississippi; L. L. Lomax, Washington, D. C.; P. B. M. Young, Cartersville, Ga.; T. L. Rosser, Charlottesville, Va.; W. W. Allen, Montgomery, Ala.; S. B. Maxey, Paris, Tex.; William Mahone, Petersburg Va.; G. W. Custis Lee, Lexington, Va.; William B. Tallaferro. Gloucester, Va.; William T. Martin, Natchez, Miss.; C. J. Polignac, Orleans, France; E. M. Law, Yorkville, S. C.; Richard Gatlin, Fort Smith, Ark.; Matt Ransom, United States senate, North Carolina; J. A. Smith, Jackson, Miss.; William H. Forney, Jacksonville, Ala.

Brigadier Generals.

George T. Anderson, Anniston, Ala.; Frank C. Armstrong, Washington. D. C.; E. P. Alexander, Savannah, Ga.; Arthur S. Bagby, Texas; Laurence S. Baker, Suffolk, Va.; Pinckney D. Bowles, Alabama; Rufus Barringer. Charlotte, N. C.; Seth M. Barton, Fredericksburg, Va.; John Bratton, White Oak. S. C.; J. L. Brent, Baltimore, Md.; C. A. Battle, Alabama; R. L. T. Beale, Hague. Va.; Hamilton P. Bee, San Antonio, Tex.; W. R. Boggs, Winston, N. C.; Tyree H. Bell, Tennessee; William L. Cabell, Dallas, Tex.; Ellison Capers, Columbia. S. C.; James R. Chalmers, Vicksburg, Miss.; Thomas L. Clingman, Asheville. N. C.; George B. Cosby, Sacramento, Cal.; Francis M. Cockrell, United States senate, Missouri; Phil Cook, Atlanta, Ga.; John B. Clark, Jr., Rockville, Md.; Alfred Cumming, Augusta, Ga.; William R. Cox, Raleigh. N. C.; Joseph Davis. Mississippi City, Miss.; H. B. Davidson, California; T. P. Dockery, New York City; Basil W. Duke, Louisville, Ky.; John Echols, Louisville. Ky.; C. A. Evans,

Atlanta, Ga.; Samuel W. Ferguson, Greenville, Miss.; J. J. Finley, Florida;
D. M. Frost, St. Louis, Mo.; Richard M. Gano, Dallas, Tex.; James Z. George,
Jackson, Miss.; William L. Gardner, Memphis, Tenn.; G. W. Gordon, Memphis,
Tenn.; D. C. Govan, Arkansas; Johnson Hagood, Barnwell, S. C.; George P. Har-
rison, Sr., Auburn, Ala.; A. T. Hawthorne, Dallas, Tex.; Eppa Hunton, United
States senator, Warrenton, Va.; William P. Hardeman, Austin, Tex.; N. H.
Harris, Vicksburg, Miss.; George B. Hodge, Kentucky; Louis Hebert, Breaux,
La.; J. D. Imboden, Southwest Virginia; Henry R. Jackson, Savannah, Ga.;
William H. Jackson, Nashville, Tenn.; Bradley T. Johnson, Baltimore, Md.;
A. R. Johnson, Burnet, Tex.; George D. Johnston, Washington, D. C.; Robert D.
Johnston, Birmingham, Ala.; J. D. Kennedy, Camden, S. C.; William H. King,
Austin, Tex.; William W. Kirkland, New York; James H. Lane, North Carolina;
A. R. Lawton, Savannah, Ga.; T. M. Logan, Richmond, Va.; Robert Lowry, Jack-
son, Miss.; Joseph H. Lewis, Frankfort, Ky.; W. H. Lewis, Tarboro, N. C.; Wil-
liam McComb, Gordonsville, La.; Samuel G. McGowan, Abbeville, S. C.; E.
McNair, Hattiesburg, Miss.; Dandridge McRae, Searcy, Ark.; John T. Morgan,
United States senate, Alabama; T. T. Mumford, Uniontown, Ala.; George Manney,
Nashville, Tenn.; B. McGlathan, Savannah, Ga.; John McCausland, Mason C. H.,
W. Va.; W. R. Miles, Mississippi; Wm. Miller, Florida; John C. Moore, Texas;
Francis T. Nichols, New Orleans, La.; R. L. Page, Norfolk, Va.; W. H. Payne,
Warrenton, Va.; W. F. Perry, Glendale, Ky.; Roger A. Pryor, New York City;
C. W. Phyfer, Mississippi; W. H. Parsons, Philadelphia, Pa.; E. W. Pettus,
Selma, Ala.; W. A. Quarles, Clarkesville, Tenn.; B. H. Robertson, Washington,
D. C.; F. H. Robertson, Waco, Tex.; George W. Rains, Augusta, Ga.; Daniel Rug-
gles, Fredericksburg, Va.; Charles A. Ronald, Blacksburg, Va.; D. H. Reynolds,
Arkansas City, Ark.; Wm. P. Roberts, Raleigh, N. C.; L. S. Ross, College Sta-
tion, Tex.; Jake Sharp, Jackson, Miss.; Joe Shelby, Carthage, Mo.; Charles M.
Shelley, Birmingham, Ala.; James E. Slaughter, Washington, D. C.; F. A.
Shoup, Sewanee, Tenn.; Thomas B. Smith, Nashville, Tenn.; G. M. Sorrell, Sa-
vannah, Ga.; George H. Stewart, Baltimore, Md.; Marcellus A. Stovall, Augusta,
Ga.; Edward L. Thomas, Washington, D. C.; W. R. Terry, Richmond, Va.; J. C.
Tappan, Helena, Ark.; Robert B. Vance, Asheville, N. C.; A. J. Vaughan, Memphis,
Tenn.; James A. Walker, Wytheville, Va.; D. A. Weisger, Richmond, Va.; C. G.
Wharton, New River, Va.; Marcus J. Wright, Washington, D. C.; G. J. Wright,
Griffin, Ga.; W. S. Walker, Florida; H. H. Walker, New York; W. H. Wallace,
Columbia, S. C.; T. N. Waul, Galveston, Tex.; John S. Williams, Mount Sterling,
Ky.; Zebulon York, Baton Rouge, La.; W. H. Young, San Antonio, Tex.; T. W.
Frazier, Memphis, Tenn.; B. H. Thomas, Atlanta, Ga.; Robert Macklay, Cook's
Landing, La.; J. R. Jones, West Virginia.

HON. JOHN H. REAGAN, OF TEXAS.

EX-POSTMASTER GENERAL OF THE CONFEDERATE STATES—THE SOLE
SURVIVOR OF PRESIDENT DAVIS' CABINET.

United Confederate Veterans.

LIST OF OFFICERS.

General John B. Gordon, general commanding, Atlanta, Ga.; headquarters during reunion at Hutchins house, Houston, Tex.

Adjutant general and chief of staff, Major General George Moorman, New Orleans, La.

Assistant adjutant general, Colonel Joseph A. Chalaron, New Orleans, La.

Quartermaster general, Major General J. F. Shipp, Chattanooga, Tenn.

Assistant quartermaster general, Brigadier General E. D. Willett, Mississippi.

Inspector general, Major General Robert F. Hoke, North Carolina.

Judge advocate generals, Major General Matthew C. Butler, South Carolina, and Major General William B. Bate, Tennessee.

Second assistant judge advocate general, Brigadier General B. F. Jonas, New Orleans, La.

Commissary general, Major General Joseph Wheeler, Alabama.

Surgeon general, Joseph Jones. M. D., Louisiana.

Second assistant surgeon general. Brigadier General Christopher Hamilton Tebault, M. D., New Orleans.

Third assistant surgeon general, Brigadier General Hunter Holmes McGuire, M. D., Richmond, Va.

Chaplain. the Rev. Thomas R. Markham, New Orleans.

LIEUTENANT GENERAL JOSEPH WHEELER.

BIOGRAPHICAL SKETCHES.

GENERAL J. B. GORDON.

OHN B. GORDON is perhaps the best type of the Confederate soldier of all men now living, in whom the most dazzling quality was personal courage. The South had no braver son than he. He once told me that when he went into the war and was called upon to face an enemy he never thought of danger. He felt that as a soldier he had a certain duty to perform, and that whether he came out of the battle alive, or was left dead upon the field, "was none of his business; the Lord would see to that!" Perhaps he was confirmed in this indifference to danger by a number of narrow escapes, which may have led him (as it has led many others) to feel that he had a charmed life. For the old hero confessed to me that after he had been struck a few times, and on one occasion carried off the field for dead, he "began to reflect" that he was not absolutely invulnerable, and perhaps it might be as well to take some precautions at least against useless exposures. That sounds like the very words of truth and soberness, and we might expect the man who used this language of prudence to behave accordingly. No doubt he made good resolutions and kept them until the next battle.

What the particular occasion was that brought him to this "realizing sense" of his danger, and to the good resolution to be more prudent afterwards, I heard from his wife. Calling at the governor's house with my friend, Mr. Samuel M. Inman, we found him just leaving for New York. He came in, however, to see us, and gave us the warmest welcome, talking in his hearty way for a few minutes till he had to leave for the train, while we lingered to enjoy what was left behind of his delightful home circle, and heard some of his experiences from one not less brave than he, who followed him in all his campaigns, and who was never far away from the sound of battle. It was on the field of Antietam (or Sharpsburg, as the Southerners call it) that General Gordon was shot five times. First he felt a sharp pain in the calf of his right leg, as if a

72

GENERAL JOHN B. GORDON.

wasp had stung him; it was a minie ball that had gone through. He
would have felt it more but he had no time to think about it, for all
around him men were falling like sheaves of grain. At such a moment all
eyes are turned upon the commander, and for him to quit the field or
show any sign of weakness might demoralize a vital portion of the
army. So he held himself erect, though he felt the blood trickling from
his wound, which soon ran faster as a second shot pierced him again,
this time a little higher on the same leg. An hour later a third ball
crashed through his left arm. Blood was streaming from three un-
staunched wounds, while a fourth ball tore through his shoulder. He
still refused to leave the field. "Tell my men," he said, "to fire on, and fire
fast. I shall not leave them." Without a bandage on a single wound,
weak and dizzy from loss of blood, he reeled along his lines, cheering
his men, when he was struck down by a fifth ball through his face (the
scar of which remains to this day), and the soldiers raised up and carried
to the rear what they supposed to be the dead body of their late commander.

Gentle reader, did you ever think you were dead? Did you ever
come so near the border land that you seemed to have floated away from
all earthly scenes, and to be in another sphere, where spirits were gliding
to and fro, and you heard voices not of this world? So it was with the
wounded soldier as he was borne from the field of battles. He was in a
half-conscious state, in which it was, as it were, at once dead and not
dead—dimly sensible of what was going on around him, and yet verging
away into the realm of the invisible. The terrible scenes in which he
had borne a part grew dim. The thunder of battle, the rush of horsemen,
the tramp of infantry, the lumbering of artillery, all grew fainter and
fainter on his ear, till he sank into that oblivion which men call death.

Then came a few hours of unconsciousness, broken only by a faint
sensation of being carried across a river (the army was retreating across
the Potomac), and then he sank again, and still was carried on and on,
till they laid him down, far away in Winchester, Va., where at last, amid
the shadowy forms around him and the whispering voices, there came a
voice that he knew, and as he opened his eyes there was bending over
him one whose coming was like that of the angel of the resurrection.

For weeks she watched by him, thinking that every day would be
the last, yet watching still, even though it were only to perform the last
offices of affection, rather than any hope of recovery. But at length the
miracle was wrought. With all his wounds he had a great natural vitality,
which kept his heart beating, till, with such nursing and such care, he
began slowly to revive, and sometimes as she sat by him, would open his
eyes and smile and utter some playful remark, which showed that the
vital spark was not extinct. And so he finally rose up to be once more

J. H. Shipp.
QUARTERMASTER GENERAL, U. C. V.

Joseph Jones, M. D.
SURGEON GENERAL, U. C. V.

Matthew C. Butler.
JUDGE ADVOCATE GENERAL, U. C. V.

a man and a soldier. As the war went on he grew in the confidence of his great chief till he became one of his most trusted lieutenants, and was almost always at his side, and so remained to the end. Indeed, on him it fell, when the last hour came, and "all was lost but honor," to tell his beloved commander that it only remained for him to submit to the last stern fate of a soldier—and surrender!

These military associations have given General Gordon an unbounded popularity among his companions in arms, the soldiers who served under him, and with the people of Georgia, who have conferred upon him the highest honors they had to bestow. It is pleasant to see honors thus come unsought; and a still further pleasure it is to think that she who followed her husband in camp and field is still at his side to share whatever honors may come to him in this golden autumn of his life.   H. M. F.

GENERAL GEORGE MOORMAN.
ADJUTANT GENERAL AND CHIEF OF STAFF, U. C. V.

MAJOR GENERAL GEORGE MOORMAN.

HE following sketch of the most important staff officer in the United Confederate Veterans' Association, is taken from one of the New Orleans papers of date July 5, 1891, where General Moorman resides:

General George Moorman, recently appointed adjutant general and chief of staff of the United Confederate Veterans by General John B. Gordon, commanding general, with his headquarters in New Orleans, is one of the best known citizens of Louisiana, having been long identified with the business interests of this city in many capacities, which has caused him to be well and favorably known in every parish and in nearly every home in the state.

His services given gratis to the state and people as president of the State Immigration Association of Louisiana, which was so conspicuously successful under the management of himself and his associates, has given him a strong hold upon the esteem and confidence of the citizens of Louisiana.

General Moorman has long been well known here and in Mississippi, where he has at different times resided, and where he is connected with some of the best families; but he has recently come into prominence through his active and energetic measures in favor of attracting and securing immigration to this state. In this important service he has proven himself able, zealous and full of resource, and probably no private citizen of Louisiana has accomplished as much in that direction. To the post of United States marshal he will bring the same zeal and activity and intelligent comprehension of his duties, and on this his friends and promoters can safely count. He and they are to be congratulated.

Previous to that he held high position on the Jackson railroad, now the Illinois Central, holding a position similar to general agent at this place; had been partner in the firm of Payne, Kennedy & Co., and J. U. & H. M. Payne & Co., and was with the "cotton king," the late Colonel Ed. Richardson, and the great cotton firm of Richardson & May, and was the promoter and connected with many enterprises for the good of

KARMA, JERVIS AND REATON DEANE.
WACO, TEXAS.

Louisiana. He was appointed United States marshal by President Cleveland, and filled the office with great satisfaction to the public and credit to himself. His family came from Lynchburg, Va., and moved to Kentucky, where he was born ,at Owensboro, June 1, 1841, and at which place he studied law, moved West, and after engaging in the Kansas war, and a trip out on the plains on foot, returned and settled in Kansas City and obtained his license to practice law in Independence, Mo., at nineteen years of age. He raised a local company, of which he was made captain, in Kansas City, for home service on the border between Missouri and Kansas. He assisted to capture Liberty Arsenal, in Clay county, and bring the arms south of the Missouri river.

He disbanded the home company, and on the approach of the Federal forces commanded by Captain Stanley (afterwards General Stanley), joined an infantry company as private and was at the engagement at Dry Creek, near Independence, where the first gun was fired west of the Mississippi river. He was made captain and aide-de-camp on the staff of General Roger Hanson Weightman, and was, at times during the war, on the staff of Generals M. Jeff Thompson, Gid. J. Pillow, Governor Thomas C. Reynolds, of Missouri, John P. McCown, Milton A. Haynes, Lloyd Tilgham, Bushrod R. Johnson, Mansfield Lovell, William H. Jackson, Wirt Adams, N. B. Forrest and Stephen D. Lee.

He served with distinction in all arms of the service—infantry, artillery and cavalry; and was successively aide-de-camp and assistant adjutant general of brigade, division, corps and department, thus eminently fitting him for the important position he now holds of adjutant general of all the United Confederate Veterans and chief of General Gordon's staff.

He was a prisoner of war three times, and when captured at Fort Donelson was taken to Camp Morton, at Indianapolis, Ind., Camp Chase, at Columbus, Ohio, and was confined in prison on Johnson's Island nearly one year.

At Fort Donelson he carried to Colonel (afterwards general) Forrest the first order he ever received to move forward into regular battle.

He was the hero of some of the most thrilling and romantic episodes of the war, notably at Fort Donelson, Coffeeville and near Sharon, Miss., and his name is specially and repeatedly mentioned for gallantry in battle in the official records of the rebellion, and the many orders there signed by him show the conspicuous and important part he acted in the great civil war at Belmont, Fort Donelson, Corinth, Sherman's Meridian Campaign, Holly Springs, Coffeeville, Franklin, Spring Hill, Columbia, Canton, Yazoo City, Birdsong's Ferry, Mechanicsburg, Harrisburg, Thompson Station, Tenn., Livingston, Miss., Jackson, Miss., around Vicksburg, Coleman's Cross Roads, and in nearly all of General W. H.

STATE REPRESENTATIVES AT THE BIRMINGHAM REUNION, U. C. V.

Jackson's battles, engagements, skirmishes, campaigns and raids, nearly a hundred in all, being almost daily engaged from the 6th of February, 1863, to March 20, 1864. He resigned from the staff on account of injury to his eyesight from constant writing and was placed in command of Moorman's cavalry battalion, with rank of lieutenant colonel, which was increased to a regiment and finally surrendered with General Dick Taylor's forces.

Just at the close of the war he married Miss Helen Shackleford, daughter of Chief Justice Thomas Shackelford, of Canton ,Miss.

He served as sheriff of Madison county, Miss., for nearly three years, during the difficult period of reconstruction, and managed the office with great ability and success, satisfying all parties. He was also engaged in planting and merchandising at the same time. He moved to New Orleans in 1869, where he has been ever since.

He conceived the idea and organized Camp No. 9, Veteran Confederate States Cavalry Association of New Orleans, Louisiana, of which he was president and commander, which position he has held for four years, and until he resigned it and declined re-election; he is also first vice president Louisiana Historical Society.

He is progressive and is a great organizer and worker, and his appointment will give satisfaction to every veteran in Louisiana. While a zealous lover of all the memories of the war, and the strongest advocate of his side, yet he urges reconciliation and fraternal feeling between the blue and gray.

The conception of and calling together the cavalry clans from every Southern state into the great cavalry reunions held in New Orleans on February 13, 1888, and on March 4, 1889, the organization of Camp No. 9, Veteran Confederate States Cavalry, and the idea of having vice presidents in each Southern state to form camps, corresponding to the major generals of divisions of the United Confederate Veterans, originated entirely with him. Nothing like it had ever been attempted in the South by any one before, and it is confidently believed that the ease with which he gathered the cavalrymen together in New Orleans in 1888 and 1889, induced the veterans to undertake the formation of and gave rise to the United Confederate Veterans.

At any rate, it is a fact that he conceived the idea; and his acquaintance being so general (having served with the troops from every state, and in so many capacities, it being asserted that he personally knows more veterans than any other living man), that he originated the Cavalry Veterans in 1888 and 1889, which was the first general body of veterans organized in the South.

As an organizer he stand without a peer, his efforts in organizing immigration matters in Louisiana and in calling the cavalrymen of the

MAY VAUGHN DUPREE.

WACO, TEXAS.

South into reunion at New Orleans, pale away before the wonderful
ability he has shown in working up the United Confederate Veteran
camps.

The United Confederate Veteran Association was formed June
10, 1889, the first reunion was held at Chattanooga, Tenn., July 3, 1890;
the second at Jackson, Miss., June 2, 1891, and very little enthusiam was
manifestetd, only thirty-three camps having been formed. General Gordon appointed him adjutant general and chief of staff in orders dated
July 2, 1891, and it was late in the fall or winter before he received all
the books and papers, and commenced active work; and although over
two years had elapsed since the date of organization and only thirty-three
camps had been formed, by the time of the third reunion, at New Orleans,
April 8, 1892, and in about six months' time, he had worked up one hundred and seventy-two camps, and at the fourth reunion, at Birmingham,
Ala., held April 25, 1894, there were five hundred and twenty camps
registered, and at the fifth reunion, at Houston, Texas, held May 22,
1895, there were six hundred and sixty-six camps, and at this writing,
seven hundred and eight, with papers and applications in for about one
hundred more.

General Moorman attributes his success to the power of General
Gordon's name, who is justly regarded as the greatest living Confederate,
and is held in the very highest veneration and esteem all over the South.

In addition to the appeal he made to his personal friends all over
the South to assist in building up the association, he performed a feat
which at once placed the cause and its objects before every veteran in the
South.

The noble address made by General Gordon upon assuming command September 3, 1889, and which is universally pronounced as one
of the most perfect and beautiful pieces of English composition extant,
had not been disseminated. He conceived the idea that this magic appeal
would stir up the old veterans if they could only read it, and make his
work a success, so he sent a copy to about two thousand newspapers, with
an appeal that they would all publish it simultaneously on the 6th day
of September, 1891; the patriotic editors did so; it was placed in the
hands and in the homes of every veteran in the South, and from that
moment the success of the United Confederate Veterans was an assured
fact.

General Moorman was twice voted thanks for his great work by the
veterans at the New Orleans reunion, and at Houston received an ovation upon motion of Lieutenant General S. D. Lee, and seconded by
General Gordon, the veterans rising and shouting, the like of which has
been accorded to very few men.

FIRST CAPITOL OF THE CONFEDERACY.
MONTGOMERY, ALA.

RICHMOND AFTER THE SURRENDER.

Major General John C. Underwood, commander, Chicago, Ill.; Colonel
Samuel Baker, chief of staff, Chicago, Ill.

— · —

MAJOR GENERAL JOHN C. UNDERWOOD.

OHN COX UNDERWOOD is the son of the late
Judge Joseph Rogers Underwood, by his second
wife, Elizabeth Threlkeld Cox. He was born in
Georgetown, D. C. During his father's public life
he was taken to and received his early education in
Bowling Green, Ky. He was sent to the high
school at Jacksonville, Ill., and afterward went to
college at Troy, N. Y., where he graduated with
distinction at the Rensselaer polytechnic institute at
the beginning of the late war. He espoused the cause of the South and
was made a first lieutenant of engineers, C. S. A., and afterward became a
lieutenant colonel of cavalry. He was in Richmond and Virginia until
the spring of 1863; then in Tennessee until captured, sick with typhoid
fever. As soon as he could be moved he was taken to Kentucky by his
father, and when able to walk was arrested and sent to prison. He was
closely confined in the military prisons at Louisville, two at Cincinnati,
and at Fort Warren in Boston harbor for over a year, and was finally
paroled by special order of President Lincoln, but remained a prisoner
until the clase of the war.

After hostilities ceased he practiced his profession as a civil engineer
and architect and did much work. He was city engineer of Bowling
Green, Ky.; of the public works of Warren county, Ky., and state engineer for periods aggregating fifteen years. He was councilman and
mayor of his city and lieutenant governor of his state (Kentucky) for
terms aggregating eight years. He was a journalist several years and
rendered effective service to the Democratic party. He is a prominent
Odd Fellow, having been grand master of Kentucky, grand representative to and officer of the sovereign grand lodge of the world for twenty
consecutive years, culminating in grand sire and generalissimo of the
order. He recruited, organized and equipped the Patriarchs Militant, the
semi-military corps of the Odd Fellows, thirty thousand strong, and com-

GENERAL JNO. C. UNDERWOOD.

COMMANDER DIVISION OF THE NORTH, U. C. V.

manded the body for nine years. In 1891 he was made commander of
the Northern divisions of the United Confederate Veterans, and com-
piled rosters of the Confederate prison dead buried in the Northern
states, and raised funds and erected a monument over the six thousand
Southern soldiers buried in Chicago. He is a pronounced Southerner
and a typical Kentuckian, is a large, determined man, liberal in his views,
possesing great energy; is courteous and soldierly in his bearing and
refined through birth and by education.

Lieutenant General S. D. Lee, commander, Starville, Miss.; Brigadier General E. T. Sykes, adjutant general and chief of staff, Columbus, Miss.

LIEUTENANT GENERAL STEPHEN D. LEE.

IEUTENANT GENERAL STEPHEN D. LEE, commanding the department east of the Mississippi, United Confederate Veterans, Starkville, Miss., was born in Charleston, S. C., September 22, 1833. His family was among the most distinguished in the state. During the Revolutionary war his great-grandfather, William Lee, was one of the forty principal citizens of Charleston confined on prison ship and sent to St. Augustine, Fla., after the city was occupied by the British. His grandfather, Judge Thomas Lee, was United States judge for South Carolina during Monroe's administration, presided during the nullification difficulties, and was a strong Union man. The grandson, upon his graduation in 1854 from the United States military academy at West Point, was assigned to the Fourth artillery, United States army, where he was first lieutenant and regimental quartermaster until 1861, when he resigned to cast his lot with the South in the civil war. Previous to the reduction of Fort Sumter he was appointed captain in the South Carolina army, and, on becoming aide-de-camp to General Beauregard, he, with Colonel Chestnut, carried the summons to Major Anderson, demanding the surrender of the fort, and later, when Anderson declined, they carried the order to open fire on the fort. After the fall of Fort Sumter Captain Lee was made quartermaster, commissary and engineer, disbursing officer for the Confederate army in Charleston. having been appointed captain in the regular army of the Confederate states. At his request he was relieved from these duties, which were distasteful to him, and went to Virginia in command of the light battery of Hampton's South Carolina Legion. He was in several fights with Federal gunboats on the Potomac; was promoted major of artillery November, 1861, lieutenant colonel and colonel of artillery; was with General Johnston in the Peninsula campaign and in the battles around Richmond. He took part in the battle of Seven Pines, Savage's Station and Malvern Hill: commanded the Fourth Virginia cavalry for six weeks, as all the field officers were wounded; was complimented by General Robert E. Lee for activity and gallantry; and commanded a battallion of artillery in General

Lee's army in the campaign against General Pope. His services at the second Manassas, or Bull Run, were brilliant and attracted the attention of the entire army. At Antietam he did conspicuous service, for which he was made brigadier general, November 6, 1863, and ordered by President Davis to Vicksburg, Miss., to take command of the garrison and batteries holding the Mississippi river at that point. Here he was signally successful in many engagements of importance, notably at the battle of Chickasaw Bayou, and subsequently in the battle of Baker's Creek, or Champion Hills, where he was greatly complimented for his gallantry. General Lee commanded a part of the entrenchments in Vicksburg near the railroad cut, and immediately after the fall of that city was exchanged.

REV. DR. W. S. PENICK.
CHAPLAIN GENERAL, DEPARTMENT EAST OF THE
MISSISSIPPI, U. C. V.

promoted major general August 3, 1863, and placed in command of all the cavalry in Missisippi, Alabama, West Tennessee and East Louisiana. When Sherman marched from Vicksburg to Meridian, Miss., with an army of thirty thousand men, General Lee hung on his front, rear and flanks with a cavalry force of two thousand five hundred men. The infantry force was not large enough to fight a battle and little opposition could be made by the cavalry force. When General Polk was sent from Mississippi to reinforce the Confederate army at Dalton, Ga., General Lee was promoted lieutenant general June 23, 1864, and assigned to the command of the department of Mississippi, Alabama, East Louisiana and West Tennessee. After the battle of Harrisburg, or Tupelo, Miss.,

GENERAL STEPHEN D. LEE.

COMMANDING DEPARTMENT EAST OF THE MISSISSIPPI, U. C. V.

General Lee was ordered to Atlanta, Ga., and assigned to the command
of Hood's old corps of infantry, Hood having relieved General Johnston
in command of the army of Tennessee.

When the battle of Nashville was fought and Hood badly routed,
Lee's corps held and repulsed the enemy at Overton Hill and in the dis-
aster his corps was the only one organized for three days after the rout.
He was wounded while with the rear guard late in the afternoon of the
day after this battle, but did not relinquish command until his corps was
relieved by an organized rear guard, composed of infantry and the cavalry corps of Forrest south of Columbia. As soon as General Lee was
sufficiently recovered from his wound, he resumed command of his corps
in North Carolina, and in time to surrender with the Confederate army
commanded by General Joseph E. Johnston.

By profession he is a planter, and is now president of the Mississippi
Agricultural and Mechanical College.

GENERAL WILLIAM L. CABELL.
COMMANDING TRANS-MISSISSIPPI DIVISION, U. C. V.

Lieutenant General W. L. Cabell, commander, Dallas, Texas; Brigadier General A. T. Watts, adjutant general and chief of staff, Dallas, Texas.

LIEUTENANT GENERAL WILLIAM L. CABELL.

WILLIAM L. CABELL, commanding trans-Mississippi department, United Confederate Veterans, was born in Danville, Va., on January 1, 1827.

He entered the United States military academy in June, 1846, and graduated in 1850. He was assigned to the United States army as second lieutenant of the Seventh infantry, and soon rose to rank of captain.

When the war was inevitable, Captain Cabell resigned from the United States army and offered his services to the Confederacy. He was at once commissioned as major by the Confederate government, and, under orders from President Davis, left on the 21st for Richmond, Va., to organize the quartermaster, commissary and ordnance departments. He remained in Richmond attending to these duties until June 1, 1861, when he was ordered to Manassas to report to General Beauregard, as chief quartermaster of the army of the Potomac.

After the battles of July 18 and 21, at Blackburn's Ford and Bull Run, General Joseph E. Johnston assumed command, and Major Cabell served on his staff until January 15, 1862, when he was relieved and ordered to report to General Albert Sidney Johnston, commanding the army of the west, for services under General Van Dorn in the trans-Mississippi department. He went with General Van Dorn to his headquarters at Jacksonport, Ark.

He was soon promoted to the rank of brigadier general and assigned to the command of all the troops on the White river, to hold the enemy in check, until after the battle of Elk Horn, which was fought on March 6 and 7, 1862. After that battle the army was transferred to the east side of the Mississippi river; the removal of this army, which included Price's Missouri and McCulloch's Arkansas, Louisiana and Texas troops, and his own command, devolved on General Cabell, and was performed in a single week from points on White river, Arkansas.

When General Bragg's army was ordered to Kentucky General Cabell was transferred to an Arkansas brigade, which he commanded in

H. W. GRABER.
QUARTERMASTER GENERAL, TRANS-
MISSISSIPPI DEPT., U. C. V.

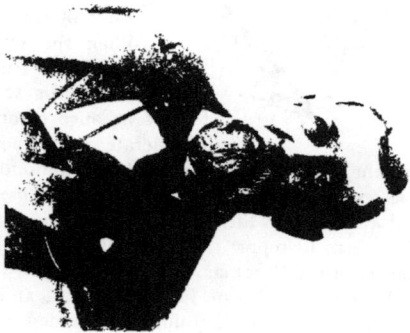

B. S. WATKIN.
AID-DE-CAMP, TRANS-MISSISSIPPI DEP'T,
U. C. V.

G. R. FEARN.
AID-DE-CAMP AND ASS'T ADVOCATE GEN.
TRANS-MISSISSIPPI DEP'T., U. C. V.

the battles of Iuka and Saltillo in September, and at Corinth on October
2 and 3, 1862, and at the Hatchie bridge on the 4th. He was wounded
leading the charge of his brigade on the breastworks at Corinth, and also
at Hatchie bridge, which disabled him from command. What was left of
his command was temporarily assigned to the First Missouri brigade,
under General Bowen.

When sufficietly recovered for duty in the field, General Cabell was,
in February, 1863, placed in command of all the forces in Northwest
Arkansas, with instructions to augment his command by recruits from
every part of that section of the state. He was very successful, and organized one of the largest and finest cavalry brigades west of the Mississippi.

A. T. WATTS.

ADJ. GEN. AND CHIEF OF STAFF, TRANS-
MISSISSIPPI DIV., U. C. V.

J. C. STORY.

ASS'T ADJ. GEN. TRANS-MISSISSIPPI
DEPARTMENT, U. C. V.

He commanded this brigade at Backbone Mountain, Poison Springs,
Bentonville, Fayetteville, Poteau River, Antoine, Prairie-de-Anne,
Elkin's Ferry, Mark's Mill, Pilot Knob, Reeves' Station, Franklin, Jef-
ferson City, Mo.; Gardner's Mills, Booneville, Lexington, Mo.; Marshall,
Mo.; Big Blue, Independence, Westport, Marias des Cygnes and numer-
ous other places in Arkansas, Kansas and Missouri.

On the raid into Missouri he was captured on the open field near
Mine creek, on October 24, 1864, and taken to Johnson's Island, in Lake
Erie, and from there to Fort Warren, in Boston Harbor, where he was
confined until August 28, 1865.

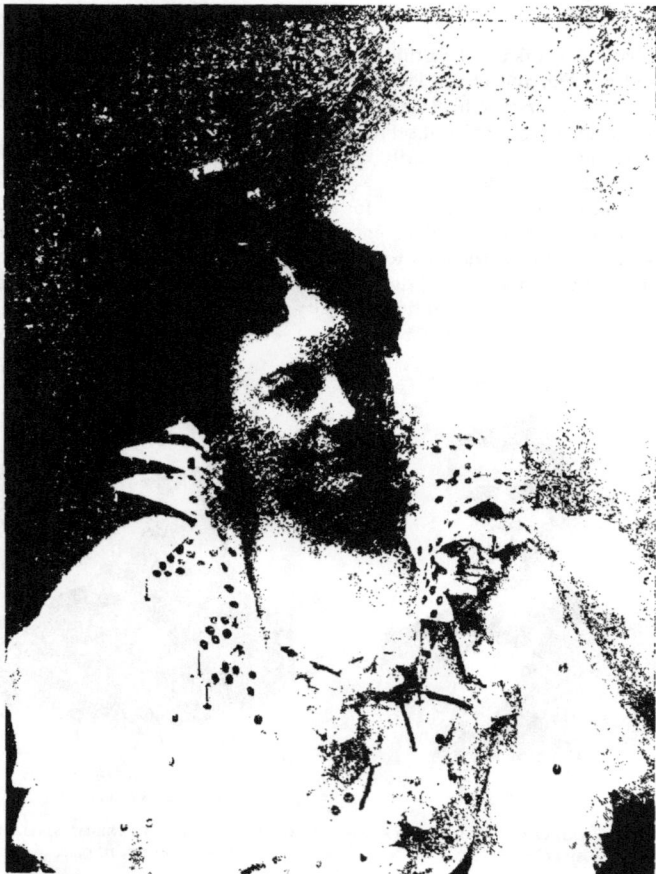

IMOGENE SAUNDERS, "QUEEN OF BELTON."

BELTON, TEXAS.

MAJOR GENERAL L. S. ROSS.

AWRENCE SULLIVAN ROSS was born in Bentons-
port, Ia., September 27, 1838. In the following spring his
father, Captain Shapley P. Ross, moved to Texas. His
early boyhood was spent surrounded by hostile Comanches and inured to hardships and dangers. In 1858, while
at home on a summer vacation from Florence Wesleyan
University of Alabama, he joined the Van Dorn campaign
with a company of one hundred and thirty-five friendly
Indian scouts and won his spurs and sobriquet of "The
Boy Captain" in a desperate battle with the Comanches,
where ninety-five of them were slain and three hundred
and fifty head of their horses were captured. In this fight
General Ross recovered from these brutal savages a little
white girl about eight years of age, whose parents were
never known, but whom General Ross brought up and
educated, naming her Lizzie Ross. A dangerous wound
received in this engagement almost put an end to his
career. He lay for five days under a post oak tree on the
battle field before he could be removed to the nearest
United States post, ninety miles distant. Before the dead were all buried
or the smoke of battle had cleared away, all the officers of the famous
Second cavalry, United States army, engaged, most of whom afterward
became prominent generals on both sides in the late war, drafted and
signed a petition to the secretary of war urging young Ross' appointment
as an officer of the regular army, and General Winfield Scott wrote him a
complimentary autograph letter, tendering his support and influence.
As Ross was not yet of age and desired to complete his college course,
he did not avail himself of the honor, but on his recovery returned to his
alma mater, where he graduated with distinction the following summer.
Immediately on his return to Texas in 1859 he was placed in command of
the frontier by the clear-sighted governor, Sam Houston, and, organizing
at once a faithful band of followers of like mettle with himself, defeated

GENERAL LAWRENCE S. ROSS.
COMMANDING TEXAS DIVISION, U. C. V.

the Comanches with great slaughter, destroying their principal village and stronghold, captured over four hundred horses and rescued Cynthia Ann Parker. In this memorable battle General Ross killed, in a hand-to-hand combat, the Chief Peta Nocona, having his horse shot down under him, but escaping without personal injury. The chief's shield, lance, buffalo horns, etc., were sent as trophies to Governor Houston, at Austin, where they were deposited in the state archives. The incidents of this struggle have been related with pride by old Texas settlers and listened to with thrilling interest by the young around many a Texas fireside, and form one of the most fascinating chapters in the history of the Lone Star state.

Entering the Confederate army as a private he rapidly rose to major, lieutenant colonel, colonel, and at the age of twenty-four was brigadier general. He participated in one hundred and thirty-five engagements of more or less importance, and had five horses shot under him, but was not wounded during the war. On different occasions he was commended to the secretary of war for gallant and meritorious conduct by Generals Joseph E. Johnston, Hardee, Forrest, S. D. Lee, Dabney H. Maury, W. H. Jackson and Van Dorn.

After the war, which left him penniless, he went to farming. In 1873 he was sheriff of his county, and as such succeeded in putting down lawlessness; in 1875 a member of the constitutional convention, and in 1881 he was elected to the state senate, in which body he served as chairman of the finance committee. Often solicited to become a candidate for governor, he only consented in 1886, when he was nominated and elected, and re-elected in 1888 by a majority of one hundred and fifty-two thousand. His record as governor is too well known to the people of the state to require comment.

He retired from this high office carrying with him the plaudits of friends and opponents; having given universal satisfaction by his conservative and patriotic policy, and he has the honor of having afforded the state one of the most popular administrations that Texas has ever had. In January, 1890, he stepped from the governor's office to the president's chair of the Agricultural and Mechanical College of Texas, where he is having ample opportunity to display his fine executive and administrative ability. As a soldier unsurpassed in gallantry, as a statesman in the foremost rank, it is now his ambition, and his versatility of genius no less qualifies him, to take a high place as an educator.

H. B. STODDARD.

ADJUTANT GENERAL AND CHIEF OF STAFF, TEXAS DIVISION, U. C. V.

M. W. SIMS.
*Asst. Quartermaster and Commissary
General.*

J. J. ADAMS.
Aid-de-Camp and A. A. General.

R. H. PHELPS.
Judge Advocate General.

S. P. MENDEZ.
Quartermaster General.

OFFICERS TEXAS DIVISION, U. C. V.

DR. R. RUTHERFORD.
Surgeon General.

DR. R. C. BURLESON.
Chaplain.

J. N. COLE.
Aid-de-Camp and Treasurer.

G. A. QUINLAN.
Aid-de-Camp.

OFFICERS TEXAS DIVISION, U. C. V.

GEO. B. ZIMPLEMAN.
Aid-de-Camp.

B. H. DAVISS.
Aid-de-Camp.

H. H. BOONE.
Aid-de-Camp.

M. F. MOTT.
Aid-de-Camp.

OFFICERS TEXAS DIVISION, U. C. V.

R. G. LOWE.
Aid-de-Camp.

THOS. D. ROCK.
Aid-de-Camp.

E. J. KELLIE.
Aid-de-Camp.

R. M. HENDERSON.
Aid-de-Camp.

OFFICERS TEXAS DIVISION, U. C. V.

J. C. J. KING, M. D.
Aid-de-Camp.

I. W. MIDDLEBROOK.
Aid-de-Camp.

W. B. SAYERS.
Aid-de-Camp.

THOS. J. GOREE.
Aid-of-Camp.

OFFICERS TEXAS DIVISION, U. C. V.

T. U. LUBBUCK.
Aid-de-Camp.

E. R. TARVER.
Aid-de-Camp.

R. N. WEISIGER.
Aid-de-Camp.

J. R. WATIES.
Aid-de-Camp.

OFFICERS TEXAS DIVISION, U. C. V.

A. L. STEELE.
Aid-de-Camp.

W. L. MOODY.
Aid-de-Camp.

J. D. SHAW.
Aid-de-Camp.

J. F. PARKS.
Aid-de-Camp.

OFFICERS TEXAS DIVISION, U. C. V.

TENNESSEE DIVISION.

General W. H. Jackson, commander, Nashville, Tenn.; Colonel J. P. Hickman, adjutant general and chief of staff, Nashville, Tenn.

GENERAL W. H. JACKSON.

AJOR GENERAL W. H. JACKSON, commanding the Tennessee division of the United Confederate Veterans, was born in Henry county, Tenn., in October, 1835. He was commanding a company of cavalry in the regular army on the breaking out of the war. He resigned his position in the regular army and cast his fortunes with the state of his birth. He was appointed a colonel of cavalry by President Davis. He was afterwards appointed a brigadier gen-

GENERAL W. H. JACKSON.
COMMANDING TENNESSEE DIVISION,
U. C. V.

JNO. P. HICKMAN.
ADJUTANT GENERAL AND CHIEF OF
STAFF, TENNESSEE DIV., U. C. V.

eral and was commanding a division of cavalry at the close of the war, which he surrendered at Gainesville, Ala., on May 10, 1865. He is now a resident of Davidson county, Tenn., and resides on the Belle Meade farm, and is owner of the celebrated Belle Meade farm and race stock.

General S. S. Crittenden, commander, Greenville, S. C.; Colonel James G. Hawthorne, adjutant general and chief of staff, Greenville, S. C.

GENERAL S. S. CRITTENDEN.

MAJOR GENERAL STANLEY S. CRITTENDEN commanding the division of South Carolina, United Confederate Veterans, is a native of his state, and is sixty-three years old. His father, Dr. John Crittenden, was one of the early settlers of Greenville. His grandfather, Nathaniel Crittenden, of Connecticut, was a lieutenant, and one of six brothers in the Continental army. The mother of General Crittenden was Miss Stanley, a member of that well known family in the old North state.

He volunteered at the first call for troops and was elected first lieutenant of a company that became part of the Fourth South Carolina regiment under Colonel J. B. E. Sloan, and participated prominently in the first battle of Manassas. This regiment and Wheat's battalion, forming Evans' brigade, on the extreme left, commenced the great battle and held the hosts of the enemy in check for two hours before being reinforced. The regiment suffered severely in killed and wounded. The day after the battle Lieutenant Crittenden received the appointment of adjutant in the place of the gallant Samuel D. Wilkes, of Anderson, who was killed. In the battle of Seven Pines, in May, 1862, when many of this gallant regiment were killed, Adjutant Crittenden was wounded by

110

LITTON HICKMAN
SECRETARY.

T. LEIGH THOMPSON
FIRST VICE-PRESIDENT.

HARRIS BROWN
SECOND VICE-PRESIDENT.

BISCOE HINDMAN
PRESIDENT.

J. B. DONELSON
TREASURER.

F. G. SMITH
SERGEANT-AT-ARMS.

BISHOP THOS. F. GAILOR
CHAPLAIN.

STATE OFFICERS TENNESSEE SONS OF CONFEDERATE VETERANS.

a minie ball in the left breast while in front of his command.   During his absence because of this wound, Governor Pickens appointed him lieutenant colonel of the Fourth regiment of Reserves then forming for the defense of the Carolina coast.   At the expiration of this service on the

GENERAL STANLEY S. CRITTENDEN.   JAS. G. HAWTHORNE.

COMMANDING SOUTH CAROLINA   ADJUTANT GENERAL AND CHIEF OF STAFF,
DIVISION, U. C. V.   SOUTH CAROLINA DIVISION, U. C. V.

coast he volunteered as a private in General Gary's mounted regiment, Hampton's famous legion, for service around Richmond.   He also served on the staff of General Gary.   After the war, General Crittenden returned to planting, but for ten years served in his state legislature as representative and as senator.

NORTH CAROLINA DIVISION.

Major General E. D. Hall, commander, Wilmington, N. C.; Colonel Janius
Davis, adjutant general and chief of staff, Wilmington, N. C.

GENERAL E. D. HALL.

ENERAL E. D. HALL, of Wilmington,
department commander of North Carolina, is very much the type of Old Hickory. He raised the first volunteer company in that section, if not in the state,
and arrived at Manassas just at the close
of that memorable victory July 21, 1861.
Soon after this he was appointed major
of the Seventh North Carolina regiment,
and so acquitted himself in the battle of New
Berne that he was elected colonel of the
Forty-sixth North Carolina, although a per-
sonal stranger, even to its officers. His regiment was put in Walker's
brigade, afterward famous as Cook's brigade, and it is said they were in

GENERAL E. D. HALL.

COMMANDING NORTH CAROLINA DIVISION, U. C. V.

113

every battle in Lee's army. General Cook was wounded several times, so that Colonel Hall, being senior colonel, had to take the command. This he did at Sharpsburg, Fredericksburg, Mary's Heights and Bristol Station. He declined the appointment of brigadier general, although A. P. Hill insisted upon it, in loyalty to his friend's (General Cook) approaching recovery. In December, 1864, he resigned active service on account of disability. After his health improved he was elected to the senate. He took strong ground, when necessary, in behalf of his people in the period of reconstruction.

Major General B. F. Eshleman, commander, New Orleans, La.; Colonel
G. A. Williams, adjutant general and chief of staff, New Orleans, La.

GENERAL B. F. ESHLEMAN.

HE present commander of the Louisiana division,
United Confederate Veterans, Major General
B. F. Eshelman, is a native of Pennsylvania. He
left his home at the age of twenty, going to New
Orleans, where he commenced his mercantile
career in the hardware establishment of Stark,
Day & Stauffer, predecessors of the well-known
firm of Stauffer, Eshelman & Co. At the breaking out of the war he enlisted in the Washington artillery, and before leaving New Orleans for
Virginia was elected the fourth captain of that battalion, which afterward
became so famous, not in the South alone, but throughout the United
States and Europe. Captain Eshelman commanded that portion of the
battalion that did such noble service at Bull Run, July 18, 1861—the first
artillery engagement of the war—bringing the Washington artillery
prominently before the army of Northern Virginia and himself to favorable notice. In this battle he was seriously wounded and thereby inca-
pacitated for several months. After returning to his command he was
placed in command of the battalion, vice Major Walton, who was promoted and assigned to duty as chief of artillery. General Eshelman remained in command of the Washington artillery until the surrender of
General Lee, having been promoted major and colonel of artillery. He
was with his command in the battles of Seven Pines, Second Manassas,
Sharpsburg, Fredericksburg, Chancellorsville, Gettysburg, Williamsport,
Drury's Bluff, Petersburg, and many others of lesser importance.

After the war General Eshelman, returning to mercantile life, soon
became a partner in the house he had served so faithfully as a clerk.

He has served as president of the New Orleans Board of Trade, Mer-
chants' and Manufacturers' Association, New Orleans Paint and Oil
Association, and has been actively associated with many social and charitable institutions.

GENERAL B. F. ESHLEMAN.
COMMANDING LOUISIANA DIVISION, U. C. V.

GENERAL THOS. A. BRANDER.
COMMANDING VIRGINIA DIVISION, U. C. V.

Major General Thos. A. Brander, commander, Richmond, Va.: Colonel Joseph V. Bidgood, adjutant general and chief of staff, Richmond, Va.

MAJOR GENERAL THOS. A. BRANDER.

EX-CONFEDERATE MAJOR THOMAS A. BRANDER, past commander of R. E. Lee camp No. 1, United Confederate Veterans; past commander of Grand Camp of State of Virginia; major general and commanding Virginia division, United Confederate Veterans, headquarters 834 East Main street, Richmond, Va., was born in the city of Richmond, Va., where he hás resided all his life. He is now fifty-five years old, and was engaged in mercantile life until the secession of Virginia, when he became a private in company F, First Virginia regiment. In April, 1861, was elected second lieutenant of company A, Twentieth regiment, Virginia volunteers, and as such participated in the battle of Rich Mountain, W. Va. On his return he was promoted to a captaincy in the provisional army of Virginia. In the latter part of 1861 he assisted in raising and equipping the "Letcher battery" of six pieces of light artillery, of which he was made junior first lieutenant, in which capacity he served until the battle of Chancellorsville, May, 1862, when he was promoted to the captaincy of of his battery. He continued to serve as captain until January, 1865, when he was promoted major of artillery and assigned to Colonel Poague's battalion, where he served until the surrender at Appomattox. He was wounded at Fredericksburg, December, 1862, and was an active participant in nearly all of the battles of the army of Northern Virginia.

MISSISSIPPI DIVISION.

Major General Robert Lowry, commander; Colonel George M. Govan, adjutant general and chief of staff, Columbus, Miss.

MAJOR GENERAL ROBERT LOWRY.

AJOR GENERAL ROBERT LOWRY, commanding the Mississippi division of United Confederate Veterans, was born in South Carolina, but when a small child his father moved to Perry (now Decatur) county, Tenn.; thence to Mississippi, where the subject of this sketch has since resided. General Lowry entered the Confederate army at the outbreak of hostilities in 1861, as a private in company B, Sixth Mississippi regiment. Upon the organization of that regiment he was elected to the position of major. After the battle of Shiloh, where he was wounded, he was promoted to the colonelcy of his regiment, Colonel Thornton, on account of wounds, having retired. In 1864 General Lowry was made brigadier general, which position he continued to hold until the termination of the war. He participated in the battles of Port Hudson, Baker's Creek, Corinth, Shiloh, Nashville, Franklin and most of the other important engagements of the army of Tennessee.

Since the cessation of hostilities he has practiced his profession, the law.

KENTUCKY DIVISION.

Major General John Boyd, commander, Lexington, Ky.; Colonel Joseph M. Jones, adjutant general and chief of staff, Paris, Ky.

MAJOR GENERAL JOHN BOYD.

AJOR GENERAL JOHN BOYD, commanding Kentucky division, United Confederate Veterans, Lexington, Ky., was born in Richmond, Ky., January 7, 1841. He is and since the war has been engaged in the saddlery business, and is a member of the firm of Thompson, & Boyd. He entered the army of the Confederate states at Lexington, Ky., in the summer of 1862, and joined the Buckner guards of Buckner's division, and later Cleburne's division, and served continuously with this division to the close of the war. He was in the battles of Murfreesboro, Chickamauga, Missionary Ridge, Ringgold Gap, the campaign from Chattanooga to Atlanta, Jonesboro, Dalton, Franklin and Nashville. He surrendered at Greensboro, N. C., May 1, 1865.

GENERAL ROBERT LOWRY,
COMMANDING MISSISSIPPI DIVISION,
U. C. V.

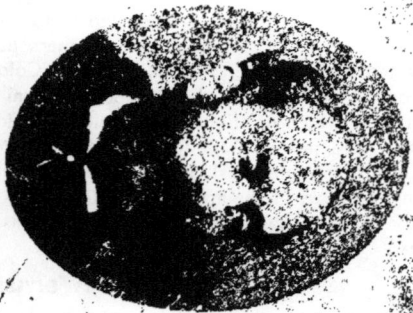

JOSEPH M. JONES,
ADJUTANT AND CHIEF OF STAFF, KEN-
TUCKY DIVISION, U. C. V.

GENERAL JOHN BOYD,
COMMANDING KENTUCKY DIVISION,
U. C. V.

Major General Fred S. Ferguson, commander, Birmingham, Ala.; Colonel Harvey E. Jones, adjutant general and chief of staff, Montgomery, Ala.

GENERAL FREDERICK S. FERGUSON.

GENERAL FREDERICK S. FERGUSON, is a native of Huntsville, Ala., was graduated at the Wesleyan University, Florence, Ala., in July, 1859, and until the war taught school and studied law. In January, 1861, he was with the expedition commanded by Colonel Lomax, which captured the navy yard and ports at Pensacola, Fla., and soon afterward was appointed second lieutenant of artillery in the regular regiment raised by Alabama and transferred to the Confederacy. Having passed the examination for a commission as an ordnance officer, he served in artillery and was staff officer to Generals Gardner, Higgins and Page. During the siege of Fort Morgan he commanded one of its batteries, with the rank of captain, and was captured with its garrison in August, 1864, from which time until June, 1865, he was a prisoner at Fort Lafayette, N. Y., and Fort Warren, Mass.

GENERAL FREDERICK S. FERGUSON.
COMMANDING ALABAMA DIVISION, U. C. V.

Major General J. J. Dickison, commander, Ocala, Fla.; Colonel Fred L. Robertson, adjutant general and chief of staff, Brooksville, Fla.

MAJOR GENERAL JOHN J. DICKISON.

MAJOR GENERAL DICKISON, commanding Florida division, United Confederate Veterans, was born in Monroe Co., Va., March 27, 1824, in the good old times when the people of that grand mountain country were in blissful ignorance of the wonderful speed of the "iron horse," and when called away from their peaceful homes on business or pleasure, were content with the quiet comfort of the old-fashioned family coach or the public stage coach. His father was a planter, so his boyhood life was a rural one. He was remarkable for his love of the military, delighted in reading the brilliant exploits of the great military leaders of history. It was the cherished hope of his father that his son—who was named for his old friend, General Jackson—should be educated at West Point, and therefore his early tastes were all so directed, but at the age of sixteen he had attained his full height of six feet, and as is the inevitable result of such rapid growth, his physical strength was impaired. He was therefore sent to South Carolina, where he found a genial climate and pleasant home with relatives. His studies were continued and the years passed quietly away without the hoped-for military training.

He entered the Confederate service as a lieutenant of artillery. On the reorganization of the army he was promoted to the captaincy. In 1863 he received a commission from Governor Milton as major general to command the state militia, but declined, as that position would have taken him out of the Confederate states' service. He was then commissioned by the governor and by Major General Sam Jones to order out the state troops whenever he saw a necessity and to discharge them when not needed. Later he received from the Confederate states government a commission as colonel of cavalry. Still later he was recommended for promotion as brigadier general, but before this was effected the war closed.

His service was confined to the state, his superior officers opposing his transfer to the Virginia, or western army. It can be justly chronicled that his gallant command was the bulwark of Florida in the years of her eventful struggle to keep back the ruthless invaders from desolating every home and happy fireside. He did his whole duty and gave his heart's best blood for the cause so dear to every heart.

The general gained the sobriquet of the "War Eagle," and was often called the "Marion of Florida," and the "Stuart of Cavalry."

A. J. WEST.

ADJUTANT GENERAL AND CHIEF OF STAFF,
GEORGIA DIVISION, U. C. V.

GENERAL J. J. DICKISON,

COMMANDING FLORIDA DIVISION, U. C. V.

GENERAL CLEMENT A. EVANS,

COMMANDING GEORGIA DIVISION, U. C. V.

Major General Clement A. Evans, commander, Atlanta, Ga.; Colonel Andrew J. West, adjutant general and chief of staff, Atlanta, Ga.

GENERAL CLEMENT A. EVANS.

ENERAL CLEMENT A. EVANS is a native of Georgia and has resided continuously in that state, except during the period of the Confederate war, when he served as a soldier in the army of Northern Virginia, commanded by General Lee. His business life began at the age of nineteen as an attorney at law, after graduating from the celebrated law school of Judge Gould, and he practiced in the courts of Southwestern Georgia with success until he entered the Confederate army. Soon after attaining the age of twenty-one years he was elected judge of the county court of Stewart county, Ga., in which he served until four years later he was elected to the senate of Georgia, where he remained until the late war begun. During his early manhood he acquired a serviceable knowledge of military tactics by belonging to the military company of his town, and thus became somewhat prepared for the duties of his after life. General Evans embraced the Southern cause with enthusiasm, and entering the service at the outset was promoted to major and then colonel Thirty-first Georgia regiment, in Lawton's, afterward Gordon's brigade. He was commissioned brigadier general and assigned to the command of the same brigade with which he had served from the date of its organization. He was engaged in the various battles of Virginia, Maryland and Pennsylvania, receiving several wounds, and several months before the close of the great struggle was promoted to the command of Gordon's division. This noted division was composed of Terry's Virginia brigade, formed by consolidation of Jones' brigade and the famous Stonewall brigade; and of Hays-Stafford's brigade from Louisiana and Evans' brigade of Georgians. General Evans commanded this division to the final surrender at Appomattox C. H. Returning home, he entered the ministry when about thirty-two years of age, and for twenty-five years filled prominent offices in his church. He has, from time to time, engaged in public affairs and conducted several important business enterprises with uniform success. Accepting the results of the war, he has urged the restoration of his state and the South to their well-deserved prosperity and absolute equality with all sections in the restored Union, and has taken advanced ground in inviting proper immigration and capital from any part of the country. General Evans is now major general of the Georgia division, United Confederate Veterans, and a member of the Historical Committee, of which General S. D. Lee is chairman.

MISSOURI DIVISION.

Major General J. O. Shelby, commander, Adrian, Mo.; Colonel H. A. Newman, adjutant general and chief of staff, Huntsville, Mo.

GENERAL J. O. SHELBY.

O. SHELBY, commander of the United Confederate Veterans in Missouri, is a Tennessean by birth and a grandson of Governor Shelby, one of the heroes of King's Mountain. He was reared in Lexington, Ky., and moved to Lafayette county, Mo., just prior to the opening of the war. He raised, armed and equipped a company and was a participant in the first battles of Missouri; Carthage, Oak Hill, Lexington and Pea Ridge, and went to Corinth after the battle of Shiloh. His activity and address attracted attention from his superior officers and he was commissioned to raise a regiment in Missouri. Taking with him his old company, he went to the Missouri river and came back to Arkansas with a full regiment, killing and capturing enough to arm and equip his command. From this on his career was remarkable, and he was to Arkansas and Missouri what Stuart was to Virginia, Forrest to Tennessee and Morgan to Kentucky. He was badly wounded at Helena, commanded a division in the Price raid in Missouri, and saved that army on its retreat to Texas. At the surrender in Shreveport of the trans-Mississippi department, he, with eight hundred of his men, withdrew and went to Mexico as exiles and sold his battery of six guns to Diaz. He took with him to Mexico Governor Isham G. Harris, of Tennessee; Governor Allen, of Louisiana, and other officers.

He subsequently returned to Missouri and lived on a farm in Bates county until appointed by President Cleveland as United States marshal for the western district of Missouri. He had refused other offices, although having them urged upon him often.

124

GENERAL J. O. SHELBY.
COMMANDING MISSOURI DIVISION U. C. V.

GENERAL JOHN G. FLETCHER.
COMMANDING ARKANSAS DIVISION U. C. V.

MAJOR GENERAL JOHN G. FLETCHER.

JOHN G. FLETCHER, major general commanding Arkansas division, United Confederate Veterans, was born in Saline county, Ark., on a farm, where he worked during crop-time and went to common country schools the remainder of the time. After arriving at his majority he went to Little Rock to live and joined a volunteer military company as a private. When the war between the states began he went with the company into the Confederate service, was at the capture of the Little Rock arsenal and the garrison of Fort Smith before the state seceded; during the summer of 1861 was in Southeast Missouri under General Hardee; from there went to Kentucky, above Bowling Green, and was in the retreat back to Corinth and was in most of the fights which the army of Tennessee was engaged in. Was promoted to first lieutenant after being out a few months and after the battle of Shiloh was promoted to the captaincy of the same company, which was company A, Sixth Arkansas infantry; was severely wounded at the battle of Stone River, or Murfreesboro, Tenn., on December 31, 1862; fell into Federal hands and remained in hospital for three months, and from there was sent to Fort McHenry, Baltimore, where he was held as prisoner of war for some time. After he was exchanged he returned to the army of Tennessee, where he remained until the surrender by order of General Joseph E. Johnston.

At the latter part of the war he served on a general court-martial for the army of Tennessee. After the war he returned to Little Rock, where he engaged in mercantile pursuits and is now engaged in banking.

126

NORTHEAST TEXAS DIVISION.

General W. N. Bush, commander, McKinney, Texas; Colonel J. M. Pearson, adjutant general and chief of staff, McKinney, Texas.

GENERAL W. N. BUSH.

N. BUSH, major general commanding the Northeast Texas division of the United Confederate Veterans, is a native of Kentucky. He was born in Clark county, May 27, 1833. He enlisted as a private in company G, Alexander's regiment of cavalry, which served in the trans-Mississippi department. Early in 1863 his regiment was removed to Louisiana and put in General Polignac's brigade, Moulton's division, where he served until the close of the war. This division did efficient service in meeting and repulsing General Banks on his expedition up Red river. The Alexander regiment captured the Nimm's battery of Banks' army. It was the first capture of cannon at Mansfield, and General Bush was the first man to reach the battery. In the second days' fight at Pleasant Hill he received a wound in the leg. In this engagement Banks was driven back to the Mississippi, but with heavy loss to the Confederates. He held the confidence of officers and comrades as a man and commander. At the close of the war he returned to his home in Collin county, Texas, and with renewed energy rebuilt his interests.

GENERAL W. N. BUSH.
COMMANDING NORTHEAST TEXAS
DIVISION, U. C. V.

J. M. PEARSON.
ADJUTANT GENERAL AND CHIEF OF STAFF,
NORTHEAST TEXAS DIVISION, U. C. V.

General William Hugh Young, commander, San Antonio, Texas : Colonel
D. M. Poor. adjutant general and chief of staff, San Antonio. Texas.

GENERAL WILLIAM HUGH YOUNG.

ENERAL WILLIAM HUGH YOUNG,
was born in Booneville, Mo., on the 1st of
January, 1838. General Young was reared
in Red River and Grayson counties. His
early education was liberal and was obtained
at Washington College, Tennessee; Mc-
Kenzie College, Texas, and the University
of Virginia, from which institution he graduated in 1861. The civil war having
begun, he remained and studied military
tactics at the university, which had been turned into
a military institute. In September, 1861, he returned to Grayson county.
Texas, and raised a company of men for the Confederate army. He was
commissioned captain, and with his company was assigned for duty
with the Ninth Texas infantry. He was in the service throughout the
war, seeing duty principally with the army of Tennessee. He was
an active participant in the great battles of Shiloh, Corinth, Perryville,
Murfreesboro, Chickamauga, Atlanta and Altoona. After the battle of
Shiloh he was made colonel of his regiment. the Ninth Texas infantry. In
1864 he was made brigadier general and as such acted the balance of the
war. At the battle of Murfreesboro he was wounded in the left shoulder
and had two horses killed under him. At Jackson, Miss., he was wounded
in the right thigh. At the battle of Chickamauga he was shot through
the left breast. At Kenesaw Mountain he was wounded in the neck and
jaw. His next service was in the Atlanta campaign—from Cassville
to Atlanta. In the battle around Atlanta General Ector, to whose brigade Colonel Young belonged, lost a leg, when Colonel Young was promoted and became its commander and was in all the subsequent engagements around and during the evacuation of Atlanta. In General Hood's
subsequent march northward French's division, to which General
Young's brigade belonged, was detached to storm Altoona Heights,
which proved to be one of the most sanguinary struggles of the war. In it
his horse was shot under him and the bones of his left ankle shot in twain.

128

In an endeavor to reach the rear he was captured by the enemy's cavalry and for four months lay in Federal hospitals in Marietta, Atlanta, Chattanooga and Nashville. In February, 1865, he was removed to Johnson's Island and there imprisoned until July 25, 1865, having been a prisoner

GENERAL W. H. YOUNG.

COMMANDING SOUTHWEST DIVISION OF TEXAS, U. C. V.

nearly ten months. General William H. Young was one of the youngest brigadiers of the Confederacy, but his war record was worthy of the bravest veteran of mature years. Since the war General Young has resided in San Antonio, Texas, engaged in the law and land business.

OKLAHOMA DIVISION.

Major General Samuel T. Leovy, commander, Norman, Oklahoma. Territory ; Colonel J. O. Casler, adjutant general and chief of staff, Oklahoma City, Oklahoma Territory.

GENERAL SAMUEL T. LEOVY.

EN. SAM T. LEOVY was born near Lexington, Ky., in 1842; was raised on a farm and received a common school education. He enlisted July, 1862, in company I, of General John H. Morgan's Kentucky regiment.

In September of that year he was appointed second lieutenant in company G, Ninth Kentucky regiment, commanded by Colonel W. C. P. Breckenridge. In 1863 the Ninth Kentucky remained under orders with the army of Tennessee, while the rest of Morgan's cavalry were on the Ohio raid. During the fall of 1863 the First, Second and Ninth Kentucky were formed into the Second Kentucky brigade, attached to General Wheeler's corps and served to the close of the war with the army of Tennessee.

On Sherman's march to the sea this brigade was very active, and did much valiant service.

December 1, 1864, Captain Leovy was dangerously wounded while leading a charge, in a cavalry fight near Bethel Church, in Brock county, Ga. His was a remarkable recovery, as he was shot through the bowels and hip. There is only one other case on record where a man received a similar wound and survived.

After the war he studied law and was admitted to the bar, but later followed his fancied occupation—stock raising and farming. In 1887 he was elected state senator for the Twenty-second Kentucky senatorial district. He located in Oklahoma City in April, 1890.

130

J. O. CASLER.

ADJUTANT GENERAL AND CHIEF OF STAFF, OKLAHOMA
DIVISION, U. C. V.

GENERAL SAMUEL T. LEOVY.

COMMANDING OKLAHOMA DIVISION, U. C. V.

WESTERN TEXAS DIVISION.

Major General E. M. Beane, commander, Cameron, Texas; Colonel W. M. McGreggor, adjutant general and chief of staff, Cameron, Texas.

— - —

ELWOOD M. BEANE.

GENERAL E. M. BEANE was born in Washington county, Md., January 5, 1839. He came to Texas in 1857 and settled in Milam county. In 1859 he was on the frontiers of Texas in the company commanded by General L. S. Ross. He enlisted in the Confederate service in the first company that went out from Milam county, which was commanded by Captain J. C. Rogers and was a part of Hood's brigade. He was in all the battles participated in by Hood's brigade up to the battle of Gettysburg, where he lost his right arm and was captured. He was a prisoner about ten months, for a while at Baltimore, a while at Fort McHenry and a while at Point Look Out, at which place he was exchanged. After he was exchanged he was placed in the invalid's corps and ordered to report to General E. Kirby Smith, but organized a battery of the reserve corps commanded by General J. B. Robertson.

After the war General Beane returned to Milam county. In 1886 he was a candidate for tax assessor of the county and was defeated by eight votes. By reason of some irregularity the Commissioner's Court threw out one small country box, which changed the result into a victory for General Beane by three votes, but he promptly declared to the court that he would not take an office upon technicalities and induced the court to reverse its action and seat his opponent. In 1888 he was elected county treasurer and twice afterward elected to the same office.

GENERAL E. M. BEANE.
COMMANDING WESTERN TEXAS DIVISION,
U. C. V.

W. M. McGREGGOR.
ADJUTANT GENERAL AND CHIEF OF STAFF,
WESTERN TEXAS DIVISION, U. C. V.

NORTHWESTERN TEXAS DIVISION.

Major General Robert Cobb, commander, Wichita Falls, Texas ; Colonel William P. Skeene, adjutant general and chief of staff, Wichita Falls. Texas.

SOUTHEASTERN TEXAS DIVISION.

Major General W. G. Blain, commander. Fairfield, Texas ; Colonel Thomas J. Gibson, adjutant general and chief of staff, Mexia, Texas.

MARYLAND DIVISION.

Major General George H. Stewart, commander. Baltimore, Md.

INDIAN TERRITORY DIVISION.

Major General N. P. Guy, commander, McAlester, I. T.; Colonel R. B. Coleman, adjutant general and chief of staff, South McAlester, I. T.

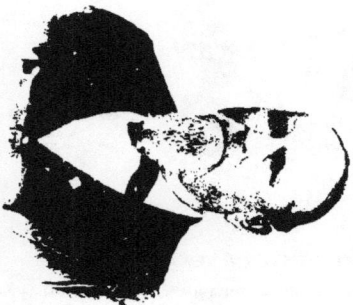

GENERAL. W. G. BLAIR,
COMMANDING SOUTHEASTERN TEXAS
DIVISION, U. C. V.

GENERAL ROBERT COBB,
COMMANDING NORTHWESTERN TEXAS
DIVISION, U. C. V.

THOS. J. GIBSON,
ADJUTANT-GENERAL AND CHIEF OF STAFF,
S. E. TEXAS DIVISION, U. C. V.

The Foremost Governors of the Southern States.

THE TROY DE @ ENG CO DE, INC.

REPRESENTATIVE TEXAS LADIES.

Miss Almeida McGregor.

WACO, TEXAS.

Miss Willie Baker.
WACO, TEXAS.

MRS. BENEDETTE B. TOBIN.
AUSTIN, TEXAS.

MISS IDA MAY ARCHER.

AUSTIN, TEXAS.

MISS ROSINE MAILLAT.

AUSTIN, TEXAS.

MISS EDNA A. FELLMAN.
GALVESTON, TEXAS.

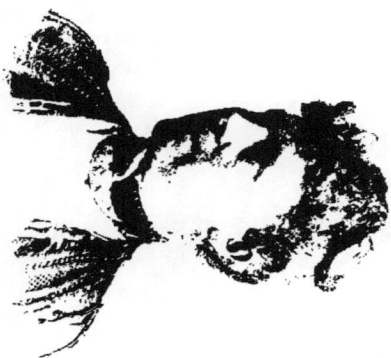

MRS. WALTER GRESHAM.
GALVESTON, TEXAS.

MISS RUBY TRAYLOR.
DALLAS, TEXAS.

MISS BLANCH FINLEY.
DALLAS, TEXAS.

MISS CLOTHILDE LASSNER.

SAN ANTONIO, TEXAS.

MRS. JOHN ADGER.

SAN ANTONIO, TEXAS.

MRS. SETH MILLER.
DALLAS, TEXAS.

MRS. J. T. MURPHY.
DALLAS, TEXAS.

MRS. SEABROOK W. SYDNOR.
HOUSTON, TEXAS,

MRS. A. H. MOHL.
HOUSTON, TEXAS.

MISS CORA ROOT.
HOUSTON, TEXAS.

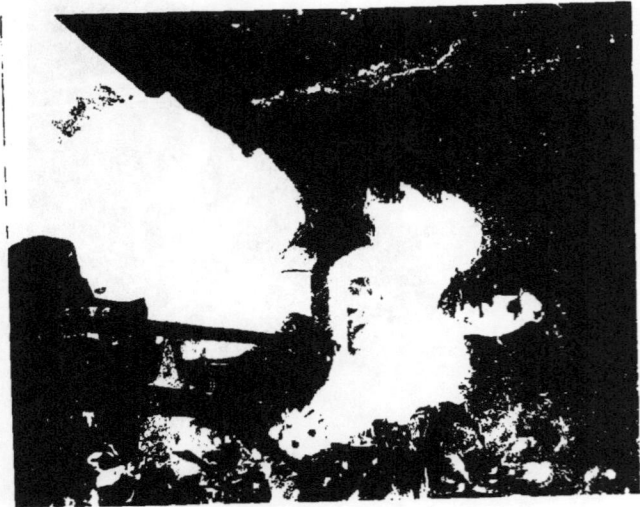

MRS. B. W. CAMP.
HOUSTON, TEXAS.

MRS. CHAS. S. HOUSE.
HOUSTON, TEXAS.

MRS. E. P. TURNER.
HOUSTON, TEXAS.

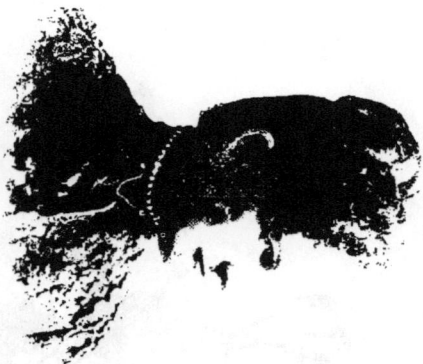

MRS. L. T. NOYES.
HOUSTON, TEXAS.

MRS. W. C. CRANE.
HOUSTON, TEXAS.

MISS JOSIE BURTON.
HOUSTON, TEXAS.

MISS MARY PORTER ROOT.
HOUSTON, TEXAS.

MISS ELLA SMITH.
HOUSTON, TEXAS.

MISS HENNIE PRICE.
HOUSTON, TEXAS.

Mrs. J. A. Huston.
HOUSTON, TEXAS.

Miss Nellie Garrett.
GALVESTON, TEXAS.

MISS NORA JANE THOMPSON.
GALVESTON, TEXAS.

MISS GRESHAM.
GALVESTON, TEXAS.

Miss Hortense Alexander.
WACO, TEXAS.

Miss Lucy Katie Lee Shaw.
WACO, TEXAS.

MISS LALIE MARSHALL.
WACO, TEXAS.

MRS. EDWARD TOBY, JR.
WACO, TEXAS.

Miss Minnie Smith.

WACO, TEXAS.

Miss Flora Cameron.

WACO, TEXAS.

MRS. R. B. DICKEY.
WACO, TEXAS.

MRS. GEORGE CLARK.
WACO, TEXAS.

OUR DIXIE.

BY A LADY OF AUGUSTA, GA., 1865.

I heard long since a simple strain:
It brought no thrill of joy or pain,
Nor did I care to hear again
          Of Dixie.

But time rolled on, and drum and fife
Gave token of a coming strife,
And called our youth to soldier life
          In Dixie.

And so our treasures, one by one,
All by the battlefield were won;
They heard at morn and setting sun
          Our Dixie.

Their blood flowed on the fresh green hill,
It mingled with the mountain rill,
And poured through vales once calm and still
          In Dixie.

The living rallied to their stand;
Their war cry was their "Native Land;"
But sadder from the lessening band
          Came Dixie.

Yet still it roused to deeds of fame,
And made immortal many a name;
It never caused a blush of shame,
          Our Dixie.

We may not hear that simple strain
Ever without a thrill of pain—
Our dead come back to life again
          With Dixie.

And if I were a generous foe,
I'd honor him whose heart's best throe
Leaped to that music soft and low,
          Our Dixie.

Mrs. C. S. Wigg.
Houston, Texas.

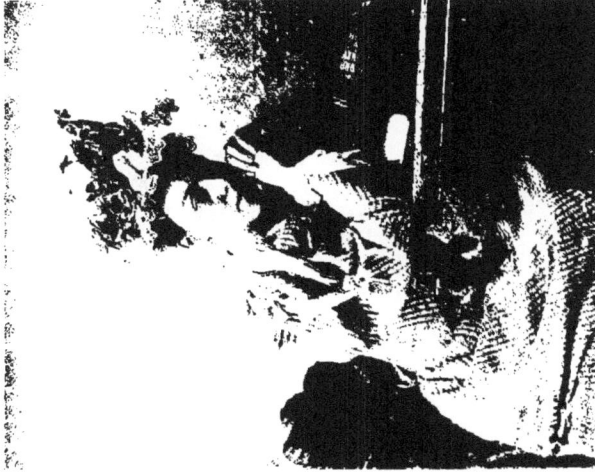

Mrs. C. H. Lucy.
Houston, Texas.

MRS. CHAS. EDWIN JONES,
HOUSTON, TEXAS.

MRS. O. T. HOLT,
HOUSTON, TEXAS.

MRS. W. B. TURNER.
HOUSTON, TEXAS.

MISS BELLE DICKSON.
HOUSTON, TEXAS.

MRS. NED WINSTEAD.
HOUSTON, TEXAS.

MRS. E. P. DAVISS.
HOUSTON, TEXAS.

MRS. RICHARD COCKE.
HOUSTON, TEXAS.

MRS. ARCHIBALD S. HALL.
HOUSTON, TEXAS.

MRS. F. CHAS. HUME.
GALVESTON, TEXAS.

MRS. E. WALTHALL HUTCHINSON.
COLLEGE STATION, TEXAS.

MISS FANILU PACE.
WACO, TEXAS.

MISS ELEANOR BAKER.
CUERO, TEXAS.

MRS. ELOISE PHILPOTT MOORE.
CUERO, TEXAS.

MISS LEONA WOODWORTH.
CUERO, TEXAS.

MISS HATTIE TRICE.
WACO, TEXAS.

MISS WILLIU TIBBS.
WACO, TEXAS.

Miss Helen Clark.
Dallas, Texas.

Mrs. Terry.
Waco, Texas.

MISS MAMIE MALONEY.

AUSTIN, TEXAS.

Miss Fannie Goggin.

Austin, Texas.

MISS IRENE PALM.

AUSTIN, TEXAS.

MISS KATIE MCKENZIE.
BRYAN, TEXAS.

MISS ANNIE DERDEN.
BRYAN, TEXAS.

MISS OLLIE WILSON
BRYAN, TEXAS.

MISS KATIE PARKER.
BRYAN, TEXAS.

A PRAYER.

(By a mother for her son, aged 15, Memphis, July 26, 1864.)

GOD bless my darling, venturous boy,
  Where'er his feet may stray;
God bless the sacred, righteous cause
  For which he went away;
God bless the little arm 'round which
  My wristlet went not tight,
Strengthen it, Lord, till it becomes
  A David's in the fight.

So young, so bright, so fair, so brave,
  To Thee, oh, God, above!
I leave the charge to shield and save
  The idol of my love.
One more to battle for the right
  Of free men to be free,
That hero's heart and child-like form,
  I dedicate to thee.

177

THE BONNIE BLUE FLAG.

BY HARRY MACARTHY.

We are a band of brothers, and native to the soil,
Fighting for our liberty, with treasure, blood and toil:
And when our rights were threatened, the cry rose near and far,
Hurrah for the Bonnie Blue Flag, that bears a single star!

Chorus.—Hurrah! Hurrah! for Southern Rights, Hurrah!
         Hurrah! for the Bonnie Blue Flag that bears a Single Star!

As long as the Union was faithful to her trust,
Like friends and like brethren kind were we and just;
But now when Northern treachery attempts our rights to mar,
We hoist on high the Bonnie Blue Flag that bears a Single Star.
                            —Chorus.

First, gallant South Carolina nobly made the stand;
Then came Alabama, who took her by the hand;
Next, quickly Mississippi, Georgia and Florida,
All raised on high the Bonnie Blue Flag that bears a Single Star.
                            —Chorus.

Ye men of valor, gather round the banner of the right,
Texas and fair Louisiana, join us in the fight;
Davis, our loved President, and Stephens, statesman rare,
Now rally round the Bonnie Blue Flag that bears a Single Star.
                            —Chorus.

And here's to brave Virginia! the old Dominion state,
With the young Confederacy at length has linked her fate;
Impelled by her example, now other states prepare
To hoist on high the Bonnie Blue Flag that bears a Single Star.
                            —Chorus.

Then cheer, boys, raise the joyous shout,
For Arkansas and North Carolina now have both gone out;
And let another rousing cheer for Tennessee be given,
The Single Star of the Bonnie Blue Flag has grown to be Eleven..
                            —Chorus.

Then here's to our Confederacy, strong we are and brave,
Like patriots of old, we'll fight our heritage to save;
And rather than submit to shame, to die we would prefer,
So cheer for the Bonnie Blue Flag that bears a Single Star.

Chorus.—Hurrah! Hurrah! for Southern Rights, Hurrah!
         Hurrah! for the Bonnie Blue Flag has gained the Eleventh
             Star!

MISS ANNIE GORMAN, OF MONTGOMERY, ALA.,

who sang " The Bonnie Blue Flag " to the delight of thousands of Confederate
Veterans at the Reunion.   Miss Gorman is Sponsor for
Camp Thomas, Montgomery. Ala.

BATTLE FLAG THIRD GEORGIA DIVISION.

THE CONQUERED BANNER.

By the REV. J. A. RYAN, Catholic Priest of Knoxville, Diocese of
Nashville, Tenn.

MUSIC BY A. E. BLACKMAR.

Furl that banner, for 'tis weary:
Round its staff 'tis drooping dreary;
　Furl it, fold it, it is best;
For there 's not a man to wave it,
And there 's not a sword to save it,
And there 's not one left to lave it
In the blood which heroes gave it;
And its foes now scorn and brave it,—
　Furl it, hide it, let it rest.

Take that banner down—'tis tattered,
Broken is its staff and shattered,
And the valiant hosts are scattered
　Over whom it floated high.
Oh! 'tis hard for us to fold it,
Hard to think there 's none to hold it,
Hard that those who once unrolled it
　Now must furl it with a sigh.

THE MISSES ANGIER, OF HUNTSVILLE, TEXAS,

who sang "The Conquered Banner" at the Winnie Davis Auditorium
during the Reunion.

Furl that banner, furl it sadly—
Once ten thousands hailed it gladly,
And ten thousands, wildly, madly,
    Swore it should forever wave,
Swore that foeman's sword could never
Hearts like their's entwined dissever,
'Till that flag would float forever
    O'er their freedom or their grave.

Furl it! for the hands that grasped it,
And the hearts that fondly clasped it,
    Cold and dead are lying low;
And the banner, it is trailing
While around it sounds the wailing
    Of its people in their woe.
For, though conquered, they adore it,
Love the cold, dead hands that bore it,
Weep for those who fell before it,
Pardon those who trailed and tore it,
And oh! wildly they deplore it,
    Now to furl and fold it so.

Furl that banner! true 'tis gory,
Yet, 'tis wreathed around with glory,
And 'twill live in song and story,
    Though its folds are in the dust:
For its fame on brightest pages,
Penned by poets and by sages,
Shall go sounding down the ages,
    Furl its folds though now we must.

Furl that banner! softly, slowly,
Treat it gently—it is holy—
    For it droops above the dead:
Touch it not, unfold it never;
Let it droop there, furled forever,
    For its people's hopes are dead.

"THE SOUTHERN CROSS."*

BY ST. GEO. TUCKER, OF VIRGINIA.

Published in 1860, a few months before the author's death.

———

Oh! say can you see, through the gloom and the storms,
  More bright for the darkness, that pure constellation?
Like the symbol of love and redemption its form,
  As it points to the haven of hope for the nation.
How radiant each star, as the beacon afar,
Giving promise of peace, or assurance in war!

Chorus.—'Tis the Cross of the South, which shall ever remain
  To light us to freedom and glory again!

How peaceful and blest was America's soil,
  'Till betrayed by the guile of the Puritan demon.
Which lurks under virtue, and springs from its coil
  To fasten its fangs in the life-blood of freemen.
Then boldly appeal to each heart that can feel,
And crush the foul viper 'neath Liberty's heel!
                              —Chorus.

———

* The Battle Flag was designed by Gen. Beauregard, adopted by Gen. Joseph E. Johnston after the first battle of Manassas, and afterward adopted by the Confederate Congress. The reason for this change was that in battle the Stars and Bars were frequently mistaken for the Stars and Stripes. It remained as the Battle Flag until the close of the war.

'Tis the emblem of peace, 'tis the day-star of hope,
   Like the sacred Labarum that guided the Roman;
From the shores of the Gulf to the Delaware's slope,
   'Tis the trust of the free and the terror of foeman.
Fling its folds to the air, while we boldly declare
The rights we demand or the deeds that we dare!
               —Chorus.

And if peace should be hopeless and justice denied,
   And war's bloody vulture should flap its black pinions,
Then gladly "To arms," while we hurl, in our pride,
   Defiance to tyrants and death to their minions!
With our front to the field, swearing never to yield,
Or return, like the Spartan, in death on our shield!

Chorus.—And the Cross of the South shall triumphantly wave
     As the flag of the free or the pall of the brave.

JAS. R. RANDALL.

Author of "My Maryland."

MY MARYLAND.

Written at Pointe Coupee, La., April 26, 1861.   First published in the
New Orleans Delta.

The despot's heel is on thy shore,
            Maryland!
His torch is at thy temple door,
            Maryland!
Avenge the patriotic gore
That flecked the streets of Baltimore,
And be the battle queen of yore,
            Maryland! My Maryland!

Hark to an exiled son's appeal,
            Maryland!
My Mother-State, to thee I kneel,
            Maryland!
For life or death, for woe and weal,
Thy peerless chivalry reveal,
And gird thy beauteous limbs with steel,
            Maryland! My Maryland!

Thou wilt not cower in the dust,
            Maryland!
Thy beaming sword shall never rust,
            Maryland!

Remember Carroll's sacred trust,
Remember Howard's warlike thrust.
And all thy slumberers with the just.
                    Maryland! My Maryland!

Come! 'tis the red dawn of the day,
                    Maryland!
Come with thy panoplied array,
                    Maryland!
With Ringgold's spirit for the fray,
With Watson's blood at Monterey,
With fearless Lowe, and dashing May.
                    Maryland! My Maryland!

Come! for thy shield is bright and strong,
                    Maryland!
Come! for thy dalliance does thee wrong.
                    Maryland!
Come! to thine own heroic throng,
That stalks with Liberty along,
And ring thy dauntless slogan-song,
                    Maryland! My Maryland!

Dear Mother! burst the tyrant's chain.
                    Maryland!
Virginia should not call in vain,
                    Maryland!
She meets her sisters on the plain—
"Sic semper," 'tis the proud refrain
That baffles minions back amain,
                    Maryland!
Arise, in majesty again,
                    Maryland! My Maryland!

I see the blush upon thy cheek,
                    Maryland!
For thou wast ever bravely meek,
                    Maryland!
But lo! there surges forth a shriek
From hill to hill, from creek to creek—
Potomac calls to Chesapeake,
                    Maryland! My Maryland!

Thou wilt not yield the vandal toll.
                Maryland!
Thou wilt not crook to his control.
                Maryland!
Better the fire upon thee roll,
Better the shot, the blade, the bowl.
Than crucifixion of the soul,
                Maryland! My Maryland!

I hear the distant thunder hum,
                Maryland!
The Old Line bugle, fife and drum,
                Maryland!
She is not dead, nor deaf, nor dumb—
Huzzah! she spurns the Northern scum!
She breathes—she burns! she'll come! she'll come!
                Maryland! My Maryland!

On May 1, 1863, the Confederate Congress adopted
this as the National Flag.

On March 4, 1865, the Confederate Congress adopted
this design as the National Flag of the Confederate
States, because the other, when limp, was too much like
a flag of truce.

THE STARS AND THE BARS.*

O, the South is the queen of all nations,
   The home of the brave and the true—
She makes no vain demonstration:
   But shows what her brave sons can do:
Her freedom and advancement they cherish—
   "Our rights, our liberties," they cry,
"To the rescue, we'll win the fight or perish,
   For the Southern boys never fear to die."

Chorus.—Then hurrah for the "Stars and Bars,"
     No stain on its folds ever be—
     Its glory dishonor never mars,
       And 'twill yet grace the land of the free.

Bring forward the tankard and fill it,
   Ye sons that are loyal and brave.
Our blood—O, how freely we'll spill it,
   We are fighting for freedom or the grave:
Our armies may be scattered and disbanded,
   Yet the wild woods we still will infest—
Yet shall fear the brave foe tho' single-handed,
   When the death rattle burst from his breast.
                 —Chorus.

* The Stars and Bars was the first flag of the Confederate States, and was adopted by the Confederate Congress at Montgomery, Ala.

Though black clouds sometimes may darken,
  And shadow the bright sunny sky;
To the rumbling of cannon we'll hearken,
Which tells of the foe as they fly.
Tho' thousands may fall stark and gory,
  Their requiem from gun and cannon mouth,
They'll win fame, freedom and glory;
  And all for the loved "Sunny South."

                              —Chorus.

I WISH I WAS IN DIXIE'S LAND.

BY DAN D. EMMETT.

I wish I was in de land ob cotton,
Old times dar am not forgotten,
　　Look away, look away, look away. Dixie Land!
In Dixie land whar I was born in,
Early on one frosty mornin',
　　Look away, look away, look away, Dixie Land!

Chorus.—Den I wish I was in Dixie--
　　　　Hooray, hooray!
　　　In Dixie land I'll took my stan'!
　　To lib an' die in Dixie
　　　　Away, away,
　　Away down south in Dixie.
　　　　Away, away,
　　Away down south in Dixie.

Ole Missus marry "Will-de-Weaber,"
William was a gay deceber
　　Look away, etc.
But when he put his arm around 'er
He smiled as fierce as a forty-pounder
　　Look away, etc.　　　　　—Chorus.

His face was sharp as a butcher's cleaber,
But dat did not seem to grieb 'er,
　　Look away, etc.
Ole Missus acted de foolish part,
An' died for a man dat broke her heart,
　　Look away, etc.　　　　　—Chorus.

Now, here's a health to de next ole Missus,
Ah! all de gals dat want to kiss us,
   Look away, etc.
But if you want to drive 'way sorrow,
Come an' hear dis song to-morrow,
   Look away, etc.   —Chorus.

Dar's buckwheat cakes and Injun batter,
Makes you fat, or a little fatter,
   Look away, etc.
Den hoe it down and scratch your grabble,
To Dixie's Land I'm bound to trabble,
   Look away, etc.   —Chorus.

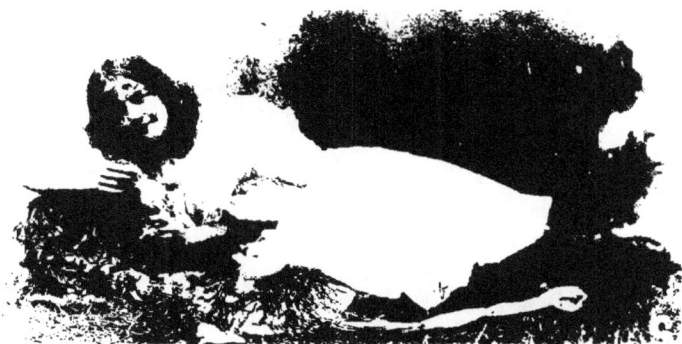

MISS FANNIE LAING, OF DALLAS, TEXAS,
who sang "Dixie" at the Reunion.

Mrs. MOLLIE E. MOORE DAVIS.
Author of " Lee at the Wilderness."

DAN D. EMMETT.
Author of " Dixie."
(PHOTO TAKEN IN 1895.)

LEE AT THE WILDERNESS.

BY MRS. MOLLIE E. MOORE DAVIS.

'Twas a terrible moment!
  The blood and the rout!
His great bosom shook
  With an awful doubt.
Confusion in front,
  And a pause in the cries:
And a darkness like night
  Passed over our skies:
  There were tears in the eyes
    Of General Lee.

As the blue-clad lines
  Swept fearfully near.
There was wavering yonder,
  And a break in the cheer
Of our columns unsteady:
  But "We are here! We are ready
With rifle and blade!"
Cried the Texas Brigade
    To General Lee.

He smiled—it meant death,
  That wonderful smile;
It leaped like a flame
  Down each close set file;
And we stormed to the front
  With a long, loud cry—
We had long ago learned
  How to charge and to die:
  There was faith in the eye
    Of General Lee.

But a sudden pause came,
  As we dashed to the foe,
And our scathing columns
  Swayed to and fro;
Cold grew our blood,
  Glowing like wine,

And a quick, sharp whisper
    Shot over our line,
As our ranks opened wide—
And there by our side
        Rode General Lee.

How grandly he rode!
    With his eyes on fire,
And his great bosom shook
    With an awful desire!
But, "Back to the rear!
    'Till you ride to the rear
We will not do battle
    With gun or with blade!"
Cried the Texas Brigade
        To General Lee.

And so he rode back;
    And our terrible yell
Stormed up to the front;
    And the fierce, wild swell,
And the roar and the rattle,
Swept into the battle
        From General Lee.

I felt my foot slip
    In the gathering fray—
I looked, and my brother
Lay dead in my way.
I paused but one moment
    To draw him aside;
Ah! the gash in his bosom
    Was bloody and wide!
    But he smiled, for he died
        For General Lee.

Christ! 'twas maddening work;
    But the work was done,
And a few came back
    When the hour was won.
Let it glow in the peerless
    Records of the fearless—
The charge that was made
By the Texas Brigade
        For General Lee.

FOLD IT UP CAREFULLY.

A Reply to "The Conquered Banner," by SIR HENRY HOUGHTON, BART., of England.

Gallant nation, foiled by numbers,
　Say not that your hopes are fled;
Keep that glorious flag which slumbers,
　One day to avenge your dead.

Keep it, widowed, sonless mothers,
Keep it, sisters, mourning brothers,
Furl it with an iron will;
Furl it now, but—keep it still,
　Think not that its work is done.

Keep it 'till your children take it,
Once again to hail and make it
All their sires have bled and fought for,
All their noble hearts have sought for,
　Bled and fought for all alone.
All alone! aye, shame the story.
　Millions here deplore the stain,
Shame, alas! for England's glory,
　Freedom called, and called in vain.

Furl that banner, sadly, slowly,
Treat it gently, for 'tis holy:
'Till that day—yes, furl it sadly,
Then once more unfurl it gladly—
　Conquered banner—keep it still!

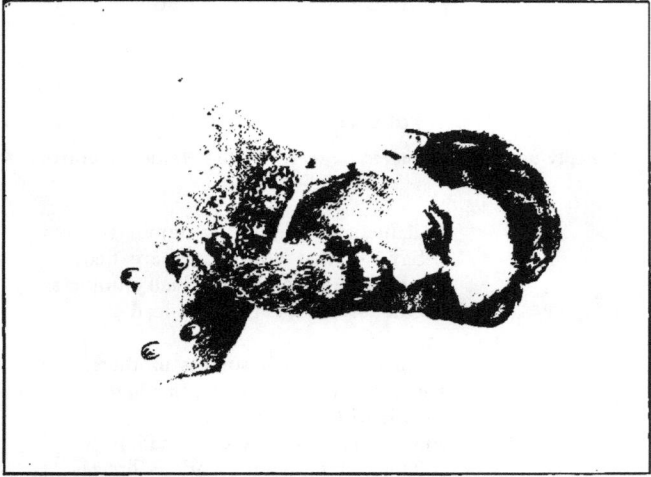

GENERAL WILLIAM J. HARDEE.

GENERAL GIDEON P. PILLOW.

THE JACKET OF GRAY.

By Mrs. C. A. Ball, Charleston, South Carolina.

Fold it up carefully, lay it aside:
Tenderly touch it, look on it with pride;
For dear must it be to our hearts evermore,
The jacket of gray our loved soldier boy wore.

Can we ever forget when he joined the brave band,
Who rose in defense of our dear Southern land,
And in his bright youth hurried on to the fray—
How proudly he donned it—the jacket of gray?

His fond mother blessed him and looked up above,
Commending to Heaven the child of her love;
What anguish was hers, mortal tongue cannot say,
When he passed from her sight in the jacket of gray.

But her country had called, and she would not repine,
Though costly the sacrifice placed on its shrine;
Her heart's dearest hopes on its altar she lay,
When she sent out her boy in the jacket of gray.

Months passed and war's thunder rolled over the land,
Unsheathed was the sword, and lighted the brand;
We heard in the distance the sounds of the fray,
And prayed for our boy in the jacket of gray.

Ah! vain, all, all vain were our prayers and our tears,
The glad shout of victory rang in our ears;
But our treasured one on the red battlefield lay,
While the life-blood oozed out on the jacket of gray.

His young comrades found him, and tenderly bore,
The cold, lifeless form to his home by the shore;
Oh! dark were our hearts on that terrible day,
When we saw our dead boy in the jacket of gray.

Ah! spotted and tattered, and stained now with gore,
Was the garment which once he so proudly wore;
We bitterly wept as we took it away
And replaced with death's white robe the jacket of gray.

THE JACKET OF GRAY.

We laid him to rest in his cold, narrow bed,
And graved on the marble we placed o'er his head,
As the proudest tribute our sad hearts could pay,
"He never disgraced the jacket of gray."

Then fold it up carefully, lay it aside,
Tenderly touch it, look on it with pride;
For dear must it be to our hearts evermore,
The jacket of gray our loved soldier boy wore!

THE VIRGINIANS OF THE VALLEY.

By FRANK O. TICHNOR.

The kindliest of the kindly band,
    Who, rarely hating ease,
Yet rode with Spottswood round the land
    And Raleigh round the seas;
Who climbed the blue Virginian hills
    Against embattled foes,
And planted there, in valleys fair,
    The lily and the rose;
Whose fragrance lives in many lands,
    Whose beauty stars the earth,
And lights the hearths of happy homes
    With loveliness and worth.

We thought they slept, the sons who kept
    The names of noble sires,
And slumbered while the darkness crept
    Around their vigil-fires.
But, aye, the "Golden Horse-shoe" knights
    Their old Dominion keep,
Whose foes have found enchanted ground,
    But not a knight asleep!

GENERAL J. A. EARLY.

GENERAL E. KIRBY SMITH.

GENERAL P. G. T. BEAUREGARD.

GENERAL BRAXTON BRAGG.

THE CONFEDERATE NOTE.*

By Miss J. Turner, of North Carolina.

Representing nothing on God's earth now,
  And naught in the water below it,
As a pledge of a nation that 's dead and gone,
  Keep it, dear Captain, and show it.
Show it to those that will lend an ear
  To the tale this paper can tell,
Of liberty born, of the patriot's dream,
  Of a storm-cradled nation that fell.

Too poor to possess the precious ore,
  And too much a stranger to borrow,
We issue to-day our "promise to pay,"
  And hope to redeem on the morrow.
Days rolled by, and weeks became years,
  But our coffers were empty still;
Coin was so rare that the treasurer quakes,
  If a dollar should drop in the till.

But the faith that was in us was strong indeed,
  And our poverty well we discerned,
And these little checks represented the pay
  That our suffering veterans earned.
We knew it had hardly a value in gold,
  Yet as gold the soldiers received it:
It gazed in our eyes with a promise to pay,
  And each patriot soldier believed it.

But our boys thought little of price or pay,
  Or of bills that were over-due;
We knew if it bought our bread to-day,
  'Twas the best our country could do.
Keep it! it tells all our history over,
  From the birth of the dream to its last;
Modest, and born of the angel Hope,
  Like our hope of success it passed.

---

* The above lines were found written upon the back of a five-hundred dollar Confederate note, subsequent to the surrender.
  The Editor would have been glad to publish an engraving of a Confederate note, but this is prohibited by the U. S. Government.

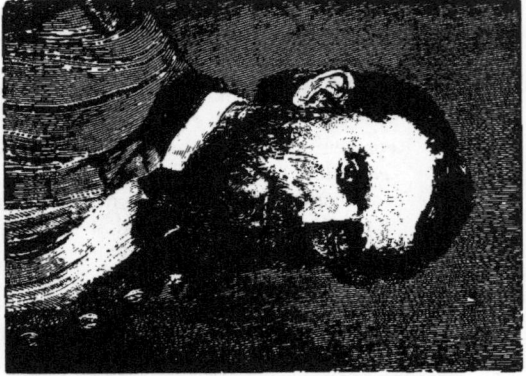

STONEWALL JACKSON.
(AT TWENTY-FOUR YEARS OF AGE.)

"Let A. P. Hill prepare for action."
(Last command of General Jackson.)

GEN. A. P. HILL.

LITTLE GIFFEN, OF TENNESSEE.

By FRANK O. TICHNOR.

Out of the focal and foremost fire,
Out of the hospital walls as dire;
Smitten of grapeshot and gangrene
(Eighteenth battle and he sixteen!),
Specter, such as you seldom see,
"Little Giffen," of Tennessee!

"Take him, and welcome!" the surgeons said;
"Little the doctor can help the dead."
So we took him, and brought him where
The balm was sweet in the summer air;
And we laid him down on a wholesome bed—
Utter Lazarus from heel to head!

And we watched the war with bated breath,
Skeleton boy against skeleton death.
Months of torture, how many such?
Weary weeks of the stick and crutch;
And still a glint of the steel-blue eye
Told of a spirit that wouldn't die.

And didn't, nay, more! in death's despite
The crippled skeleton "learned to write."
"Dear mother," at first, of course; and then
"Dear captain," inquiring about the men.
Captain's answer: "Of eighty and five,
Giffen and I are left alive.

Word of gloom from the war one day;
Johnston pressed at the front, they say.
Little Giffen was up and away;
A tear, his first, as he bade good-bye,
Dimmed the glint of his steel-blue eye.
"I'll write, if spared." There was news of the fight,
But none of Giffen. He did not write.

I sometimes fancy that, were I king
Of the princely Knights of the Golden Ring,
With the song of the minstrel in mine ear,
And the tender legend that trembles here,
I'd give the best on his bended knee,
The whitest soul of my chivalry,
For "Little Giffen," of Tennessee.

MARY A. JONES.   FRANCIS B. HOKE.
ELLEN D. HINDLE.   ADELAIDE B. SNOW.

(The four young ladies selected to ride in the procession when Jefferson Davis' body was received at Raleigh, N. C.)

PRESIDENT DAVIS' WAR RESIDENCE IN RICHMOND.

STONEWALL JACKSON'S WAY.

Found on the body of a sergeant of the Old Stonewall Brigade, Winchester, Va.

Come, stack arms, men! pile on the rails,
  Stir up the camp-fire bright;
No matter if the canteen fails,
  We'll make a roaring night;
Here Shenandoah brawls along,
To swell the Brigade's rousing song
  Of "Stonewall Jackson's way."

We see him now!—the old slouched hat
  Cocked o'er his eye, askew—
The shrewd, dry smile—the speech as pat
  So calm, so blunt, so true.
The "Blue Light Elder" knows o'er well -
Says he, "That's Banks—he's fond of shell—
Lord save his soul!—we'll give him"—well,
  That's "Stonewall Jackson's way."

Silence! ground arms! kneel all! caps off!
  Old Blue Light's going to pray;
Strangle the fool that dares to scoff!
  Attention! 'tis his way!
Appealing from his native sod,
In forma pauperis to God—
"Lay bare thine arm; stretch forth thy rod;
  Amen! That's "Stonewall's way."

He's in the saddle now! Fall in!
  Steady—the whole Brigade!
Hill's at the ford cut off! He'll win
  His way out, ball and blade;
What matter if our shoes are worn!
What matter if our feet are torn!
"Quick step—we're with him before dawn!"
  That's "Stonewall Jackson's way."

The sun's bright lances rout the mists
Of morning, and, by George,
There's Longstreet struggling in the lists,
  Hemmed in an ugly gorge—
Pope and his Yankees whipped before—
"Bayonet and grape!" hear Stonewall roar,
"Charge, Stuart! Pay off Ashby's score
  In Stonewall Jackson's way"

Ah, maiden! wait and watch and yearn
  For news of Stonewall's band;
Ah, widow! read with eyes that burn
  That ring upon thy hand;
Ah, wife! sew on, pray on, hope on,
Thy life shall not be all forlorn—
The foe had better ne'er been born,
  Than get in "Stonewall's way."

THE SWORD OF ROBERT LEE.

By Father Ryan.

Forth from its scabbard, pure and bright,
    Flashed the sword of Lee!
Far in front of the deadly fight,
High o'er the brave in the cause of Right,
Its stainless sheen, like a beacon light.
    Led us to victory.

Out of its scabbard, where, full long,
    It slumbered peacefully,
Roused from its rest by the battle's song,
Shielding the feeble, smiting the strong,
Guarding the right, avenging the wrong,
    Gleamed the sword of Lee.

Forth from its scabbard, high in air
    Beneath Virginia's sky—
And they who saw it gleaming there,
And knew who bore it, knelt to swear
That where that sword led they would dare
    To follow—and to die.

Out of its scabbard! Never hand
    Waved sword from stain as free,
Nor purer sword led braver band,
Nor braver bled for a brighter land,
Nor brighter land had a cause so grand,
    Nor cause a chief like Lee!

Forth from its scabbard! How we prayed
    That sword might victor be:
And when our triumph was delayed,
And many a heart grew sore afraid,
We still hoped on while gleamed the blade
    Of noble Robert Lee.

Forth from its scabbard all in vain
    Bright flashed the sword of Lee;
'Tis shrouded now in its sheath again,
It sleeps the sleep of our noble slain,
Defeated, yet without a stain,
    Proudly and peacefully.

ALL QUIET ALONG THE POTOMAC TO-NIGHT.

By Lamar Fontaine.

"All quiet along the Potomac to-night!"
  Except here and there a stray picket
Is shot, as he walks on his beat, to and fro,
  By a rifleman hid in the thicket.

'Tis nothing! a private or two now and then
  Will not count in the news of a battle;
Not an officer lost! only one of the men
  Moaning out, all alone, the death-rattle.

"All quiet along the Potomac to-night!"
  Where soldiers lie peacefully dreaming;
And their tents in the rays of the clear Autumn moon,
  And the light of their camp-fires are gleaming.

A tremulous sigh, as a gentle night wind
  Through the forest leaves slowly is creeping;
While the stars up above, with their glittering eyes,
  Keep guard o'er the army while sleeping.

There's only the sound of the lone sentry's tread,
  As he tramps from rock to the fountain,
And thinks of the two on the low trundle bed,
  Far away, in the cot on the mountain.

His musket falls slack, his face, dark and grim,
  Grows gentle with memories tender,
As he mutters a prayer for the children asleep,
  And their mother—"may heaven defend her!"

The moon seems to shine forth as brightly as then—
  That night, when the love, yet unspoken,
Leaped up to his lips, and when low-murmured vows
  Were pledged to be ever unbroken.

Then drawing his sleeve roughly over his eyes,
  He dashes off tears that are welling;
And gathers his gun closer up to his breast,
  As if to keep down the heart's swelling.

He passes the fountain, the blasted pine tree,
  And his footstep is lagging and weary;
Yet onward he goes, through the broad belt of light,
  Towards the shades of the forest so dreary.

Hark! was it the night-wind that rustled the leaves?
  Was it moonlight so wondrously flashing?
It looked like a rifle: "Ha, Mary, good-by!"
  And his life-blood is ebbing and splashing.

"All quiet along the Potomac to-night!"
  No sound save the rush of the river;
While soft falls the dew on the face of the dead,
  And the picket's off duty forever.

LEE TO THE REAR.

Dawn of a pleasant morning in May
Broke through the Wilderness, cool and gray,
While, perched in the tallest tree tops, the birds
Were carrolling Mendelssohn's "Songs Without Words."

Far from the haunts of men remote,
Where the brook brawled on with a liquid note,
And Nature, all tranquil and lovely, wore
The smile of Spring, as in Eden of yore.

Little by little, as daylight increased
And deepened the roseate flush on the East,
Little by little did morning reveal
Two long, glittering lines of steel.

Where two hundred thousand bayonets gleam,
Tipped by the light of the earliest beam,
And the faces are sullen and grim to see
In the hostile armies of Grant and Lee.

All of a sudden, ere rose the sun,
Pealed on the silence the opening gun;
A little white puff of smoke there came,
And anon the valley was wreathed in flame.

Down on the left of the rebel lines,
Where a breastwork stands in a copse of pines,
Before the rebels their ranks can form,
The Yankees have carried the place by storm.

Stars and stripes o'er the salient wave,
Where many a hero has found a grave,
And the gallant Confederates strive in vain
The ground they have drenched with their blood, to regain.

Yet louder the thunder of battle roars,
Yet a deadlier fire on their column pours;
Slaughter infernal rode with Despair,
Furies twain through the smoky air.

Not far off, in the saddle, there sat
A gray-bearded man, with a black slouch hat;
Not much moved by the fire was he—
Calm and resolute Robert Lee.

Quick and watchful, he kept his eye
On two bold rebel brigades close by;
Reserves, who were standing—and dying—at ease
Where the tempest of wrath toppled over the trees.

For still, with their loud bull dog bay,
The Yankee batteries blazed away,
And with every murderous second that sped,
A dozen brave fellows, alas! fell dead.

The grand old beard rode to the space
Where Death and his victims stood face to face,
And silently waved his old slouch hat,
A world of meaning there was in that.

"Follow me! Steady,—we'll save the day;"
This is what it seemed to say;
And, to the light of that glorious eye,
The bold brigades thus made reply:

"We'll go forward; but you must go back,"
And they moved not an inch in the perilous track
"Go to the rear and we'll give them a rout"—
Then the sound of the battle was lost in their shout

Turning his bridle, Robert Lee
Rode to the rear.—Like the waves of the sea,
Bursting the dykes in their overflow,
Madly his veterans dashed on the foe.

And backward in terror that foe was driven,
Its banners rent and its columns riven,
Wherever the tide of battle rolled,
Over the Wilderness, wood and wold.

Sunset, out of crimson sky,
Streamed o'er a field of ruddier dye,
And the brook ran on with a purple stain,
From the blood of ten thousand foemen slain.

Seasons have passed since that day and year,
Again o'er the pebbles the brook runs clear,
And the fields in a richer green are dressed,
Where the dead of the terrible conflict rest.

Hushed is the roll of the rebel drum,
The sabres are sheathed and the cannon are dumb;
And Fate, with a pitiless hand, has furled
The flag that once challenged the gaze of the world;

But the fame of the Wilderness fight abides,
And down into history grandly rides,
Calm and unmoved as in battle he sat,
The gray-bearded man with the black slouch hat.
                                        —THOMPSON.

ᴿEMINISCENCES.

WORSLEY'S LINES TO GENERAL LEE.

The lines to General Lee, which have been several times improperly
attributed to Lord Derby, were really written by Prof. Philip Stanhope
Worsley, of Oxford, and were first published by me in my "Personal
Reminiscences, Anecdotes, and Letters of R. E. Lee," copied from the
original, which I have seen many times in General Lee's home in Lexington, Va.

I send also two letters from General Lee to Prof. Worsley, which I
found copied in his private letter book, when after his lamented death
I had the privilege of examining and culling from the private papers of
the great chieftain. The extracts are as follows:

The following inscription and poem accompanied the presentation of a
perfect copy of the "Translation of the Iliad of Homer into Spencerian Stanza,"
by Philip Stanhope Worsley, Fellow of Corpus Christi College, Oxford, a
scholar and poet whose untimely death, noticed with deepest regret throughout
the literary world in England, has cut short a career of the brightest promise:

To General R. E. Lee, the most stainless of living commanders, and, except
in fortune, the greatest, this volume is presented with the writer's earnest
sympathy and respectful admiration.

> The grand old bard that never dies,
> Receive him in our English tongue!
> I send thee, but with weeping eyes,
> The story that he sung.
> Thy Troy is fallen, thy dear land
> Is marred beneath the spoiler's heel.
> I cannot trust my trembling hand
> To write the things I feel.
> Ah, realm of tombs! but let her bear
> This blazon to the last of times;
> No nation rose so white and fair,
> Or fell so pure of crimes.
> The widow's moan, the orphan's wail,
> Come round thee; yet in truth be strong!
> Eternal right, though all else fail,
> Can never be made wrong.
> An angel's heart, an angel's mouth,
> Not Homer's, could alone for me
> Hymn well the great Confederate South,
> Virginia first, and Lee.
>
> P. S. W.

GENERAL ROBERT E. LEE IN 1862.

"He possessed every virtue of other great commanders without their vices. He was a foe without a hate, a friend without treachery, a soldier without cruelty, and a victim without murmuring. He was a public officer without vices, a private citizen without wrong, a neighbor without reproach, a Christian without hypocrisy, and a man without guile. He was Cæsar without ambition, Frederick without tyranny, Napoleon without selfishness, and Washington without reward. He was obedient to authority as a servant, and royal in authority as a true king. He was gentle as woman in life, modest and pure as a virgin in thought, watchful as a Roman Vestal in duty, submissive to law as Socrates, and grand in battle as Achilles." —BEN HILL.

General Lee's Reply.

Lexington, Va., February 10, 1866.

Mr. P. S. Worsley—My Dear Sir: I have received the copy of your translation of the "Iliad," which you so kindly presented to me. Its perusal has been my evening's recreation, and I have never enjoyed the beauty and grandeur of the poem more than as recited by you. The translation is as truthful as powerful, and faithfully reproduces the imagery and rhythm of the bold original.

The undeserved compliment to myself in prose and verse, on the first leaves of the volume, I receive as your tribute to the merit of my countrymen who struggled for constitutional government.

With great respect, your obedient servant,   R. E. LEE.

Another Letter from General Lee.

Lexington, Va., March 14, 1866.

Mr. P. S. Worsley: My Dear Mr. Worsley—In a letter just received from my nephew, Mr. Childe, I regret to learn that, at his last accounts from you, you were greatly indisposed. So great is my interest in your welfare that I cannot refrain, even at the risk of intruding upon your sick room, from express-ing my sincere sympathy in your affliction. I trust, however, that ere this you have recovered and are again in perfect health. Like many of your tastes and pursuits, I fear you may confine yourself too closely to your reading; less mental labor and more of the fresh air of heaven might bring to you more comfort and to your friends more enjoyment, even in the way in which you now delight them. Should a visit to this distracted country promise you any recreation, I hope I need not assure you how happy I should be to see you at Lexington. I can give you a quiet room and careful nursing and a horse that would delight to carry you over our beautiful mountains. I hope my letter informing you of the pleasure I derived from the perusal of your translation of the "Iliad," in which I endeavored to express my thanks for the great compliment you paid me in its dedication, has informed you of my high appreciation of the work.

Wishing you every happiness in this world, and praying that eternal peace may be your portion in that to come, I am, most truly, your friend and servant,

R. E. LEE.

The friendship between the quiet scholar and the great soldier forms a beautiful episode in their lives. The exquisite poem of Worsley is a touching tribute to the Confederacy and to Lee, and it would seem a pity that Lord Derby or any one else should rob the poet of his laurels.

Mosby and Sixteen of his Men who Elected to stay with him until Death.

1, Colonel John S. Mosby ; 2, Norman V. Randolph ; 3, Alfred Babcock ; 4, John Puryear ; 5, Frank Rahm ; 6, Walter Gosden ; 7, Harry T. Sinnott ; 8, —— Butler ; 9, Neely Quarles ; 10, —— Newell ; 11, —— Gentry ; 12, Tom Booker ; 13, John W. Munson ; 14, —— Jordon ; 15, Bob Parrott ; 16, Ben Palmer ; 17, Lee Howerson.

The photograph from which the above engraving was made was taken in Richmond, June, 1865. The seventeen men were a part of the seventy-five who decided to remain with Mosby when they found that he and two of his scouts, Chas. McDonough and Nick Carter, were not

THE CONFEDERATE WOMEN.

What They Did During the Times of the Terrible War.

THE history of the war would not be complete without a tribute to the Confederate women. It would be injustice to them to say that they were simply patriotic; for, while they were of all patriots the greatest, they gave the Southern cause the benefit of much more than their good wishes. No women at any time in the history of the world ever surrendered as much for a cause as did the women of the South. There have been instances where hundreds have indeed made every sacrifice, but this is the only instance where a nation of women worked and fought for a nation. There was undoubtedly not one woman in the entire South during the last year of the war of whom it could be said she lived in luxury. The wife of the president of the Confederacy sold her family silver for the cause.

The invalid wife of the general of the Confederate army spent her small strength in knitting socks for the Confederate soldiers. Little girls occupied their hours in picking lint for Confederate soldiers' wounds. Saints—good, beautiful, patient, cheering, they proved angels on battle fields and in the hospitals. They starved at home in order to send their scanty food to the army. Worn and broken by privation, they wrote letters beaming with hope and gladness to the camp and resounding with defiance to the foe. No country ever had such loving daughters, no cause such tireless champions. They were the last to be reconstructed. Some of them have never been reconstructed. Some of them never will be reconstructed.

Mrs. Sallie Chapman Gordon-Law.

"MOTHER OF THE CONFEDERACY."

It would require an entire volume to tell of the unnumbered deeds of charity
during the war, of this most distinguished
Tennessee lady.

HENRIETTA H. MORGAN, MOTHER OF HEROES.

Born in Lexington, Ky., December 5, 1805; died there September 7, 1891; wife of Calvin C. Morgan, who was born December 16, 1801, and died May 1, 1854.

Mrs. Henrietta Hunt Morgan was the mother of the following sons and daughters:

John H. Morgan, major general division of cavalry, born June 1, 1825; and killed at Greenville, Tenn., September 4, 1864.

Thomas H. Morgan, lieutenant Company I, Second Kentucky Cavalry, born May 7, 1844; killed at Lebanon, Ky., July 5, 1863.

Francis Key Morgan, private Company A, Second Kentucky Cavalry, born August 23, 1845; died October 6, 1873.

Calvin C. Morgan, captain on staff of General Morgan, born June 4, 1827; died July 19, 1882.

Mrs. Kitty G. Forsythe, widow of Lieutenant General A. P. Hill, who was killed at Petersburg, April 2, 1865.

Mrs. Henrietta H. Duke, wife of Brigadier General Basil W. Duke.

Richard C. Morgan, colonel Fourteenth Kentucky Cavalry.

Charlton H. Morgan, captain staff of General Morgan.

Her life was embittered by many sorrows, but rewarded by the blessings which are given those who find happiness in good done to others. Unselfish, charitable, self-sacrificing, heroic in devotion to duty, untiring in the offices of affection, her name and memory are sanctified. She gave all her life to her family and friends. She gave her children to her country. She ministered unceasingly to the poor and helpless, and she loved the Lord her God with all her heart and all her soul and all her mind, and has "crossed over the river to rest under the shade of the trees."

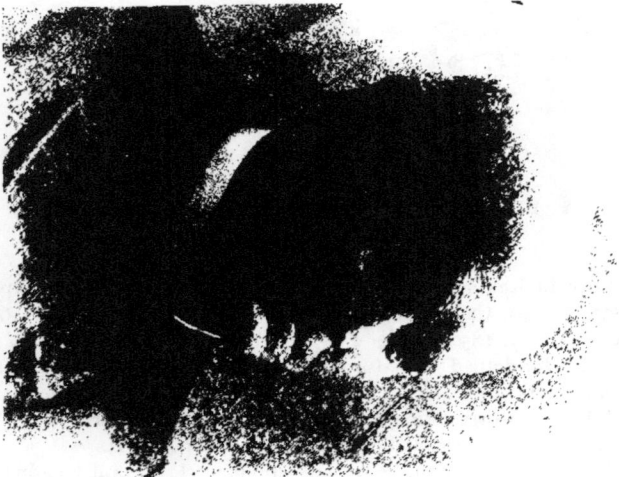

DR. S. H. STOUT.
SURGEON OF HOSPITAL.

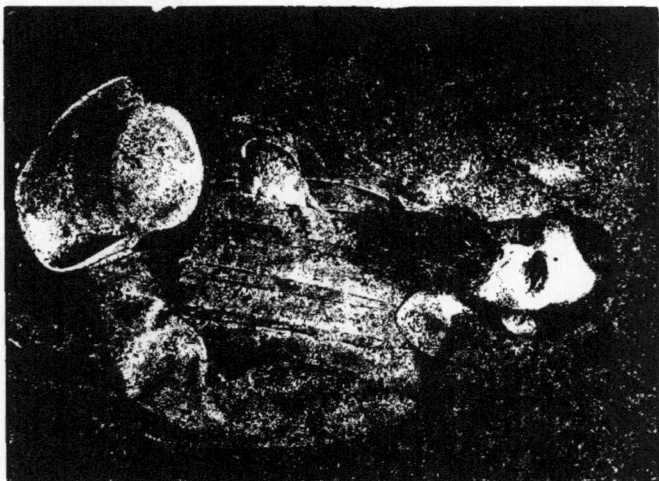

GENERAL MAHONE IN WAR TIMES.

FLORIDA WHITE.

THIS distinguished woman was Miss Ellen Adair, one of the seven daughters of General Adair, who was governor of Kentucky. At the age of eighteen she married Joseph Monroe White, who represented the Land of Flowers in the United States congress. She became eminently prominent in Washington society, and traveled with her husband throuh Europe in their private carriage. Mr. White was a leading Spanish land lawyer, and a single fee sometimes approximated $100,000. He was proud of his wife and lavish in expenditure for her pleasure and popularity. Bulwer read to her in manuscript his "Last Days of Pompeii." On their departure for return to America, Madame Murat asked Mrs. White what she could give her as a token of remembrance, and the reply came, "Your hand." That famously beautiful hand was cast in bronze and was given by the recipient to the editor of the Veteran.

Justice Story and other members of the United States supreme court paid her these high tributes:

Thou hast gone from us, lady, to shine
  Midst the throng of the gay and the fair;
If thou'rt happy, we will not repine,
  But, say, canst thou think of us there?

Circled round by the glittering crowd,
  Who flatter, gaze, sigh, and adore.
I would ask, if I were not too proud,
  Hast thy heart room for one image more?

Forgive us, dear lady, ah, do,
  We will blot out those words from our song;
Though absent, we know thou art true;
  Though jealous, we feel we are wrong.

Some millions of insects might pass
  In thy rays as those of the sun,
Then is it not folly to ask
  Thy glances should beam here alone?

222

The following is credited to John Quincy Adams:

Come bring the cap and bring the bells,
  And banish sullen melancholy,
For who shall seek for wisdom's cells
  When Ellen summons him to folly?

And if 'twere folly to be wise,
  As bards of mighty fame have chanted,
Whoever looked at Ellen's eyes
  And then for sages' treasures panted?

FLORIDA WHITE.

O, take the cap and bells away,
  The very thought my soul confuses,
Like Jack between two stacks of hay,
  Or Garrick's choice between the Muses.

Thus Apama, of beauteous renown,
  Made the proudest of monarchs grow meek;
On her own pretty head placed his crown,
  And then tapped the old king on the cheek.

Notes from Mr. Josiah Quincy's "Figures of the Past:"

MR. QUINCY'S first party in Washington was at Mrs. Wirt's, where he went in company with Mr. and Mrs. Webster, which event he emphasizes "because of meeting Mrs. White, a lady whose beauty was the admiration of Washington and whose name was, consequently upon every tongue." * * * It is said that because of some strictures upon her father, General Adair, Mrs. White controverted with Andrew Jackson some questions about the battle of New Orleans, whereby she was victor. It is perhaps the only defeat "Old Hickory" every suffered.

Five years after the death of Mr. White she was married to Dr. Beatty, whom she survived nearly forty years. Of the large estate that she possessed when the war began, there were two hundred negroes, whom she had taught to read and write. She was an aunt of General Patton B. Anderson, of Confederate fame, and of Major Butler P. Anderson, who gave his life for his fellow-men in nursing yellow fever patients years ago at Grenada, Miss.

There has evidently been no woman so highly honored in American history as Mrs. Ellen Adair Beatty, so often quoted by authors two generations ago as "Florida White." A remarkable circumstance in her career was her reception by the Pope of Rome and his gift of a magnificent diamond cross, with which she parted after the war in her liberality toward the erection of a Southern Presbyterian church in Washington City, of which Rev. Mr. Pitzer has been the pastor since its dedication.

In Mrs. Ellet's "Court Circles of the Republic" she reports an entertainment during John Quincy Adams' administration, in which she refers to Mrs. White as follows: "There was also the wealthy and magnificent Florida belle, Mrs. White, with a numerous train of admirers, a dozen orange blossoms in her hair, the wild light of the gazelle in her dark eyes, and her bust cased in glittering silver, languishing through the crowd, who retired to the right and left to permit her to pass. If met, said an admirer, walking through an orange grove in Florida, or beside a limpid lake amid the eternal spring, she would instantly become an object of worship."

At another time (Jackson's administration): "The lady usually called Mrs. 'Florida' White, because her husband, Colonel White, represented Florida, was celebrated for magnificent beauty and intellectual accomplishments throughout the Gulf States."

Her part in the war is not given in this appropriate place, but no woman in our favored Southland was more loyal and zealous from first to last. She and Mrs. James K. Polk were devoted friends. The latter was pleased to recall in the later years of their lives the eminence of her Presbyterian sister when both were in the prime of young womanhood and conspicuous at Washington.—Confederate Veteran.

CONFEDERATE MONUMENT IN CHICAGO, DECORATION DAY, 1895.

MRS. LOULIE M. GORDON, ATLANTA, GA.

RS. GORDON is the youngest daughter of a Confederate major, the wife of the youngest captain in the Confederate army, and sister-in-law of one of the most celebrated of Confederate generals. Her husband, Walter S. Gordon, raised and commanded a company at fifteen. He was afterwards on the staff of General C. A. Evans, who was ardently devoted to him, and testifies to his "absolute fearlessness, originality, and clear-headedness." The proud wife and daughter of these worthy men says she belongs with the Confederates. While she is happy in her Atlanta

MRS. LOULIE M. GORDON.

home with her two young daughters, Lute and Linda, thirteen and eight, the mother is so full of life and hope that she has become very prominent, especially in literary circles.

MRS. JENNIE CATHERWOOD BEAN.

"OUR LADY" OF THE CLARK COUNTY, KENTUCKY, CONFEDERATE
VETERAN ASSOCIATION.

The only epitaph she desires is: "She never forgot the Confederate soldiers on
tented field, behind prison bars, nor under the sod.

MRS. MAGGIE DAVIS HAYES.

Born in Washington during the latter part of her father's service as secretary of war, she is the eldest daughter, and remembers much of the trials of her father during the Confederate struggle. While Mr. Davis was in prison, Maggie was with her grandmother, Mrs. Howell, near Montreal, Canada, in the convent of the Sacred Heart at school. After Mr. Davis' release from prison she was with the family in London, and at school in England until she finished her collegiate course.

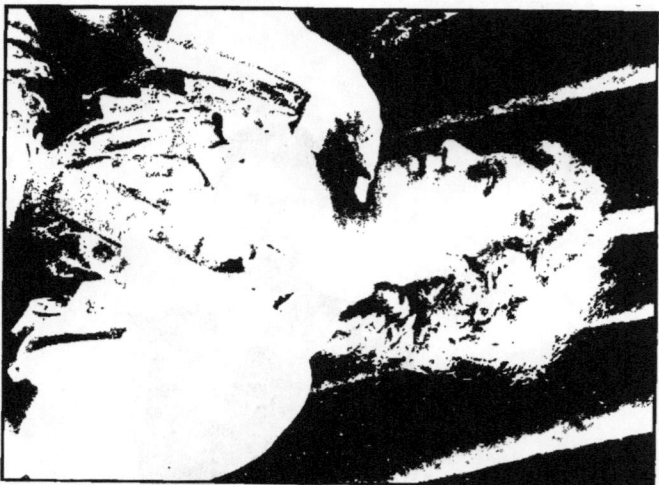

Miss Bessie B. Henderson,
Salisbury, N. C.

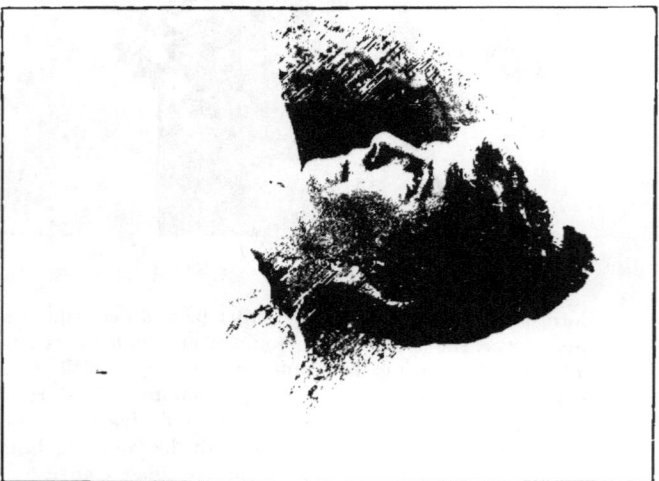

Mrs. J. M. Kickey,
of Missouri.

TWO PATRIOTIC SOUTHERN LADIES.

HEROIC SAM DAVIS.

BOUT thirty-one years ago Samuel Davis, a young Confederate soldier—but a lad, not out of his teens —while on a furlough, seeing his parents in Giles county, Tenn., was arrested by Federal troops. He had in his possession valuable papers and plans which he obviously intended to carry back to the Confederates. The information was betrayed to him by a Union soldier. Young Davis was told he would be released if he would tell who gave him the plans; otherwise he would be hanged as a spy. The boy refused to give the name of the recreant soldier, and his enemies carried

SAMUEL DAVIS MONUMENT.
ERECTED BY HIS FATHER.

GRANDSON OF JEFFERSON DAVIS.

His name was changed by legislative enactment from Jefferson Davis Hayes to Jefferson Hayes Davis.

out their threat. He was hanged in the presence of thousands of troops and in the sight of weeping people of Pulaski and the vicinity.

A writer in the Nashville Banner, F. H. Crass, a member of the old Rutherford Rifles, says:

"I can see him standing on the scaffold, about to suffer an ignominious death; his piercing dark eyes, full of manly pride, rejecting the offer made by a human enemy. Easily could he have given up the secret that was buried with him, never to be made known until the final judgment, and in so doing could have saved the life that to him, even as he stood there facing death, must have held out so many bright promises. He gave up kind parents, sisters, brothers, wealth and all and died the greatest hero of the grand and bloody drama."

Here indeed was a strain of courage, a height of virtue human being never excelled. There ought to be a monument to the boy in every cemetery of our soldier dead. Surely when it was entered upon the Book of Life, the recording angel must have kissed the name of Samuel Davis. —Huntsville Tribune.

WILLIAM DAVIS HAYES.

"I AM A *Confegorate.*"

A TOUCHING STORY OF A LITTLE SOUTHERN GIRL.

She was a tiny maid of three, but she sat upright on the cushioned seat of the well-filled passenger coach with a certain majesty and grace that pleased the more thoughtful travelers, who stopped now and then to hear her quaint, childish prattle. She was unconscious of any interest she had awakened, and told story after story of her home, dolls, playmates, and games to the lady with whom she was traveling. Then she grew con-

fidential and climbed into her companion's lap, and this gave a place at their sides to the gentleman who wished to join them a moment later. The tiny bit of precious humanity noticed, in her quick, intelligent, sympathetic way, that an empty sleeve hung at the gentleman's right side, but she looked out of the window, apparently lost in thought. After a while she spoke, but her eyes seemed still to regard the passing scene: "My farver's farver was in the war, and one day when they had a battle he saw

234

MRS. MAGGIE HAYES AND WINNIE DAVIS.
THE TWO SURVIVING CHILDREN OF JEFFERSON DAVIS.

MRS. JULIA JACKSON CHRISTIAN.
DAUGHTER OF STONEWALL JACKSON.

ever and ever and ever so many poor men, who had little chillun at home,
killed wite there before his eyes; and they was bewied wite there, and
nobody could tell their names, and their little chillun never could see
them any more." She never seemed to see the empty sleeve, but the gentleman was conscious she had done so, and that the dear little mind had
tenderly grasped the truth, that he was one of those who had been "in the
war," and that his arm had been left with the unnamed dead on some battle field—maybe the one where her "farver's farver" had fought. As he
rose to leave the train he kissed the child, and the little one's companion
saw a tear on his furrowed cheek. Are there angels who gather tears
such as this for chaplets of pearls in heaven? Then what celestial seas
of tears from our great war of sacrifice for principle!—Confederate
Veteran.

MISS MARY ELIZABETH CHIPLEY.
MISS CHARLIE CHIPLEY JONES.   MISS MARY ELLISON AIKIN.
GRANDDAUGHTER OF COLONEL THOS. II. HUNT.

A GROUP FROM PENSACOLA, FLA.

ORLEANS CADETS. *They Messed Together and Drank from the Same Canteens.*

WALTER H. ROGERS.   WALTON FRY.   WILLIAM H. RENAUD.

J. W. NOYES.   ALEX. H. CLARK.   CORNELIUS YOUNG.   JNO. K. RENAUD.

ORLEANS CADETS.

WALTER H. ROGERS.   WALTON FRY.   WILLIAM H. RENAND.
J. W. NOYES.   ALEX. H. CLARK.   CORNELIUS YOUNG.   JNO. K. RENAND.

COLONEL WILLIAM P. RODGERS.

AMONG all the great names of Texas heroes around which memory delights to linger, not one is more worthy of praise than that of Colonel William P. Rodgers, who fell in the Confederate charge at the battle of Corinth, October 4, 1862.

All civilized people take a delight in perpetuating the name and memory of their countrymen who have achieved greatness, and especially of those who have fought and died for others. Colonel W. P. Rodgers and those other brave Texans who fell at Corinth have raised for themselves monuments which will last as long as our now forever united republic; in that great effort of war they have secured memorials of themselves which neither the unkindness of the elements nor the neglect of men can either destroy or impair. So far, therefore, the fame of these heroes of Corinth is assured; but it would be only a fitting tribute to their memory that a beautiful statue or a towering monument should be erected over their graves, so that the name of Rodgers and his comrades of the Second Texas may be more frequently on the lips of the coming generations. It would be only a just recognition of their valor and a deserved token of undying love and comradeship.

More than three decades have passed since those now lying in death's embrace bade adieu to loved ones at home, to flash their maiden swords; and how well their work was done, how faithfully every duty performed, is attested by the victories they achieved, the defeats they so bravely suffered, and the immortality which is theirs. No bosom in which beats a Southern heart can fail to swell with pride at thoughts of their glorious achievements and their self-sacrificing valor. "In the garden of our hearts their fame forever shall endure."

COLONEL WILLIAM P. RODGERS.

CONFEDERATE MONUMENT, ALEXANDRIA, VA.

ALL honor to the women and men who close by the capital of the nation have erected a superb monument to their own Confederate dead at Alexandria, Va. It is surmounted by a soldier, hat in hand, his arms folded, and standing with his head a little drooped, as if he was preparing to make another vigorous battle—a battle with conditions which mean the recovery of fortune, and redemonstrating merit to distinction as a patriot. An old paper says: "For all time will Alexandria bear in her heart of hearts the manner of these gallant men who, on the 24th day of May. 1861, left their homes at the call of public duty, for the monument is inscribed with the names of those Alexandrians whose homes never saw them again, but the hearts of whose fellow-citizens will enshrine them forever:

> Yon marble minstrel's voiceless stone
> In deathless song shall tell,
> When many a vanished year has flown,
> The story how you fell;
> Nor wreck, nor change, nor winter's blight,
> Nor time's remorseless doom,
> Can dim one ray of holy light
> That gilds your glorious tomb.

"Names of scores who went from Alexandria and never returned are engraved. Other inscriptions on the monument are: 'Erected to the memory of the Confederate dead of Alexandria, Va., by their surviving comrades, May 24, 1889.' On the south face and on the north face the words: 'They died in the consciousness of duty well performed.'"

241

CONFEDERATE MONUMENT, ALEXANDRIA, VA.

Representative
Ladies of the South.

MISS TEBAULT.   MISS GIFFEN.   MISS FANCHILD.   MISS PERSONS.

REPRESENTATIVE YOUNG LADIES OF NEW ORLEANS.

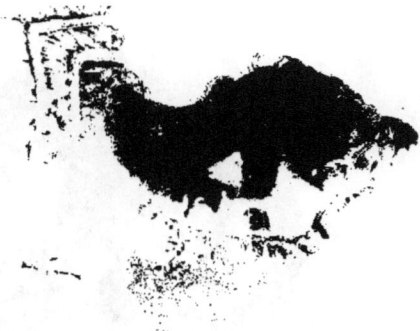

MISS REBECCA DUN RENNY,
MONTGOMERY, ALA.

MISS MAMIE GREIL,
MONTGOMERY, ALA.

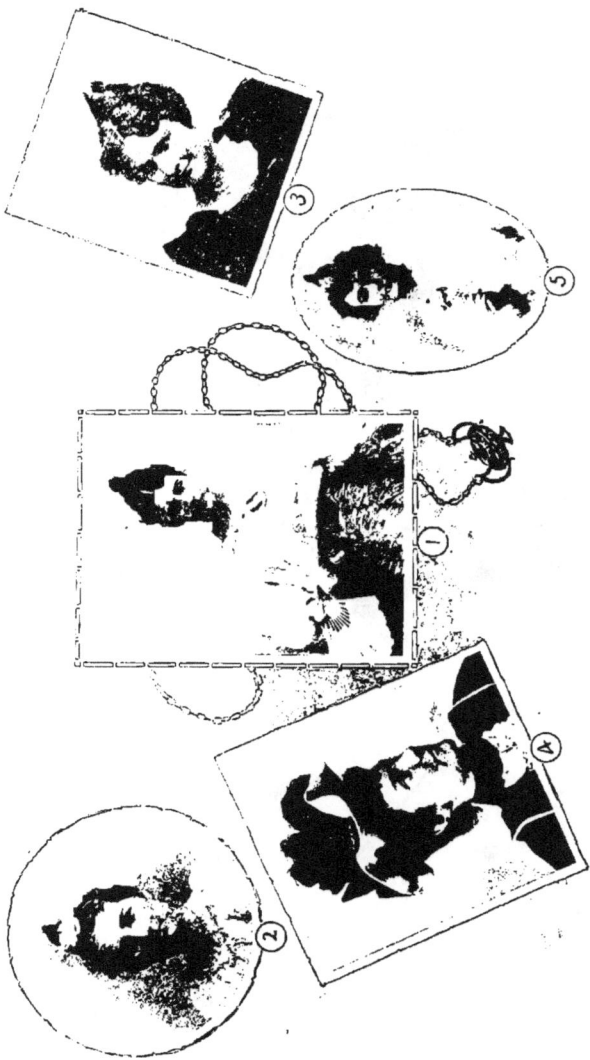

1   MISS ALINE OLTORF.
2   MISS ELLEN GARDNER.

3   MISS JONNIE POWERS.

SOCIETY GROUP, MARLIN, TEXAS.

4   MISS IRENE IRMA JONES.
5   MISS MAMIE CANOLA.

1 MISS GEORGIE GILKESON.
2 MISS EUGENIA GAY DAVIS.

3 MISS BESSIE SHELBY HUSTON.

SOCIETY GROUP, LEXINGTON, MISSOURI.

4 MISS MAUD MULLER BURDEN.
5 MISS SARA BAY McCLELLAND.

MISS JANET ESTES.
MEMPHIS, TENN.

MISS DAISY B. NEELY.
MEMPHIS, TENN.

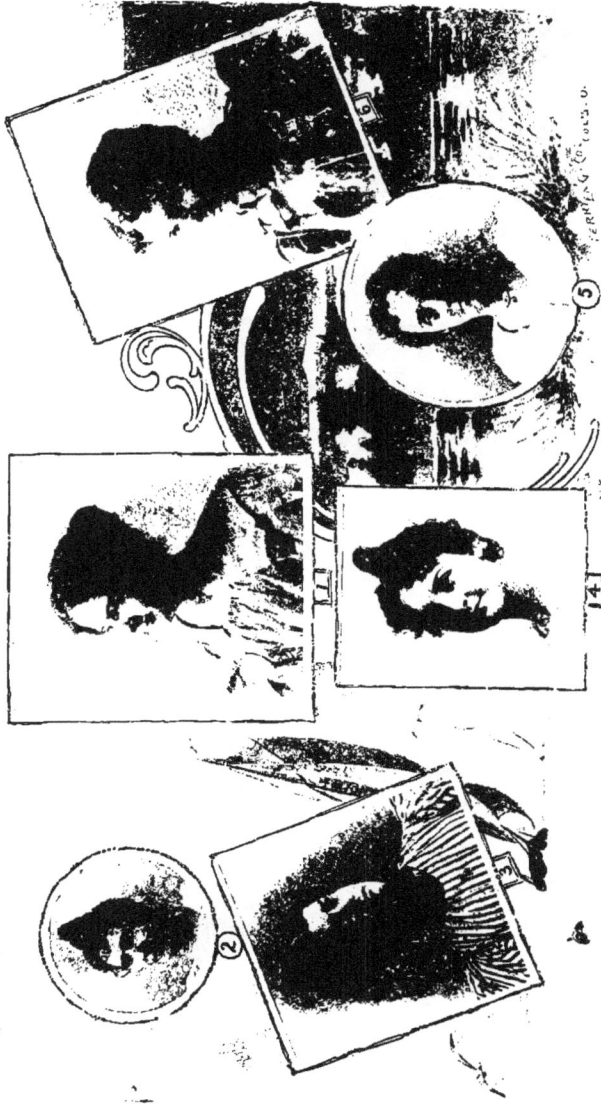

1 MISS GABYE LEVY.
2 CLARE V. PRESCOTT.

3 MISS ETHEL BLANCHARD.
4 MISS T. OLIVE FOSTER.

5 MISS LUCILLE FOSTER.
6 MISS MAMIE BOOTH.

SOCIETY GROUP, SHREVEPORT, LOUISIANA.

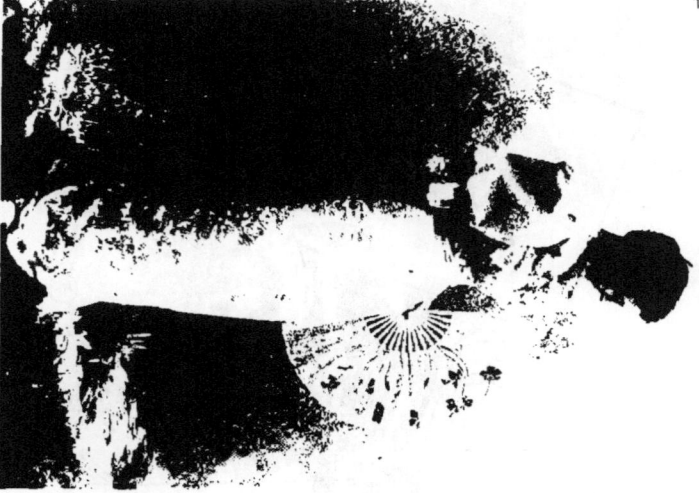

MISS ANNIE HELEN REESE.
BIRMINGHAM, ALA.

MISS MARY CROMMELIN.
MONTGOMERY, ALA.

MISS FRANCIS SHOBER.
SALISBURY, N. C.

MISS JANIE SOUTHERLAND SMITH.
DANVILLE, VA.

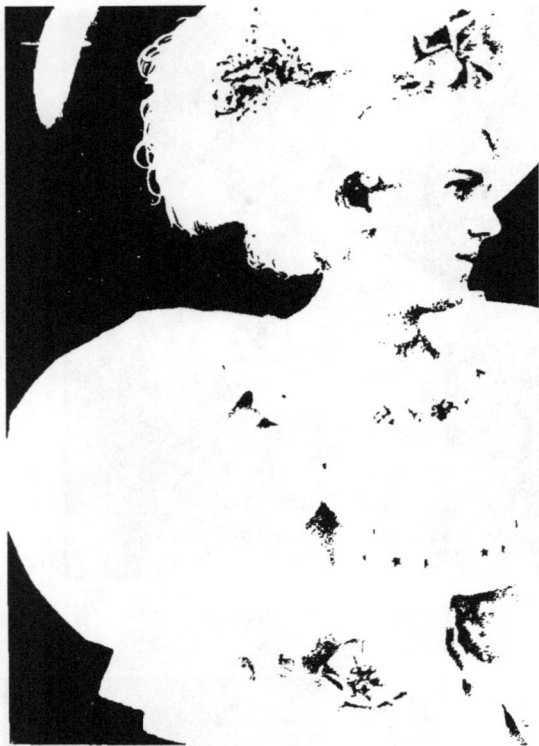

MISS IRENE ELOISE MOOTY.

COLUMBUS, GA.

Miss Nina Peabody.
COLUMBUS, GA.

Miss Mattie D. Houstoun.
TALLAHASSEE, FLA.

Miss Annie Fair.
MURFREESBORO, TENN.

1 MISS ALICE McFARLANE.
2 MISS ELIZABETH STRONG.

3 MISS ALICE HENDERSON.
4 MISS RUTH EVANS.

5 MISS FANNIE MAE BURKS.
6 MISS VELA WINN.

SOCIETY GROUP, LA GRANGE, GEORGIA.

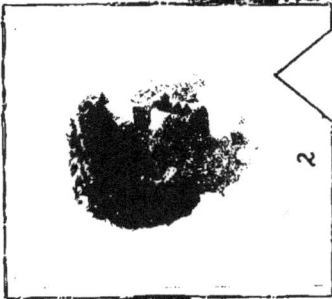

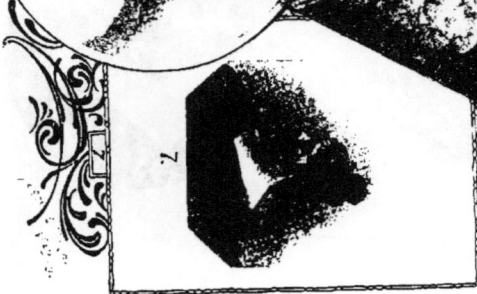

1 MISS LOCKE FRANCES ARNOLD.
2 MISS ALICE MOUNTJOY.

3 MISS BESSIE COHR.
4 MISS MINNIE NEALE.
5 MISS FLORENCE GLENN.

6 MISS MARY CHEW.
7 MISS SUSAN ARNOLD McCAUSLAND

DAUGHTERS OF CONFEDERATE VETERANS, LEXINGTON, MISSOURI,

Sponsors
and
❖ Maids of Honor ❖

United

Confederate Veteran

Camps

MISS HATTIE DUVAL HARN,

SPONSOR FOR STATE OF TEXAS.

MISS HATTIE DUVAL HARN, State Sponsor for the Division of Texas, is the daughter of Captain Tyder D. Harn, who came from Maryland to Texas in 1859, and served in the Confederate Army from 1861 to the close of the war.

When Colonel Mott, of General Ross' staff, transmitted to Miss Harn the staff badge, he assured her that she had been made by special order of General Ross, an honorary member of his staff an honor that was happily bestowed by the chivalrous general and highly valued by the young lady.

Miss Harn is a native Texan, as is also her mother.

1 MISS LIZZIE CAIN, CALVERT, TEXAS. 2 MISS EVA MYERS, LOCKHART, TEXAS. 3 MISS WINNIE PARKER, BRYAN, TEXAS.

MAIDS OF HONOR TO MISS HARN, SPONSOR FOR STATE OF TEXAS.

Miss Virginia Leoma Cobb, Wichita Falls, Texas.
SPONSOR FOR NORTHWESTERN TEXAS DIVISION.

Miss Ella Gordon Robinson, Cameron, Texas.
SPONSOR FOR WEST TEXAS DIVISION.

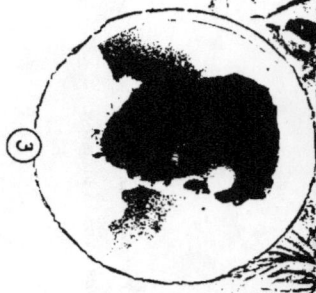

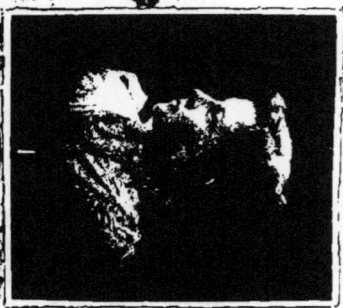

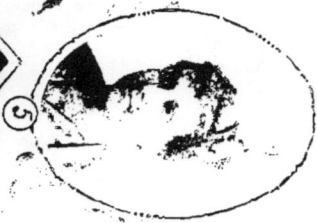

McIntosh Camp No. 361, Chico, Texas.

1 Miss Emma L. Blanton, Sponsor, Chico, Texas.
2 Miss Josephine Eddins, Maid of Honor,   "   "
3 Miss Della Watson,   "   "   "

Haskell, Co. Confed. Vet. Camp No. 633, Haskell, Texas.

1 Miss Minnie Lindsey, Sponsor, Haskell, Texas.
2 Miss Fannie Gillespie, Maid of Honor,   "   "
3 Miss Eugenia English,   "   "   "

R. E. Rodes Camp, Quanah, Texas.

1. Miss Lollie Harwell, Sponsor, Quanah, Texas.
2. Miss Maud Banks Patterson, Maid of Honor.
3. Miss Alice Evans, "

Winnie Davis Camp No. 108, Waxahachie, Texas.

1. Miss Mai Boyce, Sponsor, Boyce, Texas.
2. Miss Blanche Coley, Maid of Honor.

R. E. LEE CAMP, FORT WORTH, TEXAS.

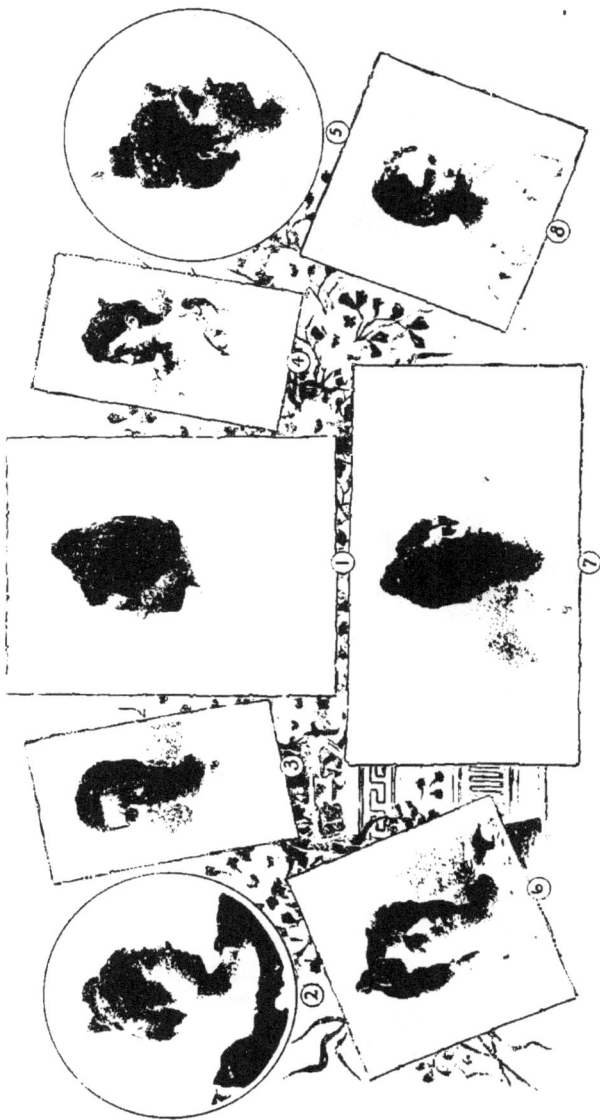

MAGRUDER CAMP NO. 105, GALVESTON, TEXAS.

JOHN B. GREGG CAMP NO. 587, LONGVIEW, TEXAS.

2 MISS EUGENIA SCOTT, MAID OF HONOR.   1 MISS LENORE E. YOUNG, SPONSOR,   4 MISS TILLIE D. HARTMAN, MAID OF HONOR.
3 MISS ANNA L. HOSKINS, " "   LONGVIEW, TEXAS,

ALBERT SIDNEY JOHNSTON CAMP NO. 144, SAN ANTONIO, TEXAS.

1 MISS ERNESTINE C. KROEGER, SPONSOR,
   SAN ANTONIO, TEXAS.
2 MISS MARY POOR, MAID OF HONOR.
3 MISS ADA WALLACE, MAID OF HONOR.
4 MISS ADELAIDE LUBY,   "   "
5 MISS KATIE PACK, MAID OF HONOR.
6 MISS MAMIE LUBY,   "   "
7 MISS MABEL MUSSEY,   "   "

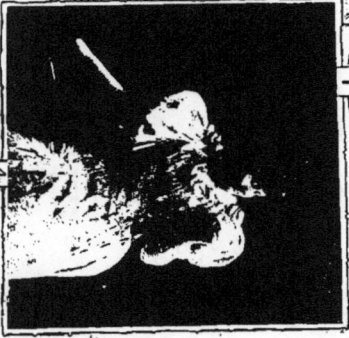

WINKLER CAMP NO. 147, CORSICANA, TEXAS.

1 MISS ANNIE CLAIBORNE WOOD, Sponsor, CORSICANA, TEXAS.

2 MISS MYRA WINKLER, MAID OF HONOR.
3 MRS. A. V. WINKLER, CHAPERON.

3 MISS BETTIE HARPER, MAID OF HONOR.
4 MISS KATIE L. DAFFAN, "
5 MISS ZETTA MORSE, "

SCOTT ANDERSON CAMP No. 619, EAGLE LAKE, TEXAS.

1 MISS MAGGIE PUTNEY, MAID OF HONOR. 2 MISS MAGGIE E. DAVIDSON, SPONSOR, 4 MISS ERNA ANDERSON, MAID OF HONOR.
3 MISS GEORGIE NORRIS, " " EAGLE LAKE, TEXAS. 5 MISS MOLLIE CONNOR, " "

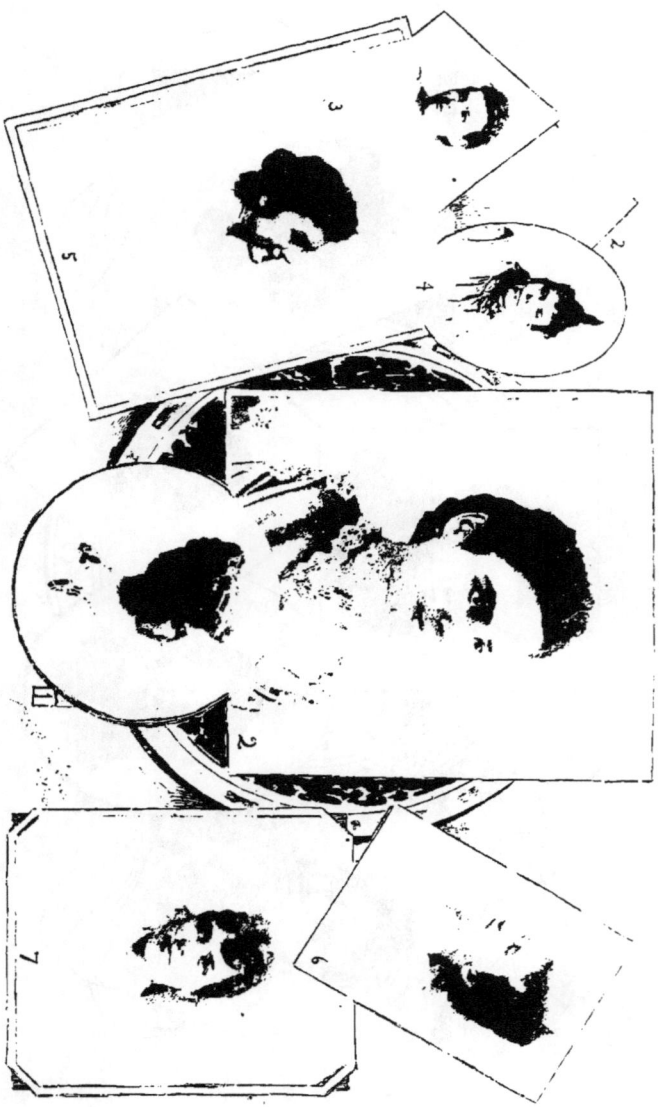

EMMETT LYNCH CAMP No. 242, CUERO, TEXAS.

2 MISS MATILDA HUNTER, MAID OF HONOR.   1 MISS KATIE LORD, SPONSOR,   5 MISS MITCHIE WOFFORD, MAID OF HONOR.
3 MISS LILY HUNTER,   "   "   CUERO, TEXAS.   6 MISS INOGENE CALHOUN,   "   "
4 MISS DELIA WRIGHT,   "   "   7 MISS RUTH WARE,   "   "

MOUNTAIN REMNANTS CAMP No. 536, BURNET, TEXAS.

1 MISS KATHARINE BLACKBURN, SPONSOR, BURNET, TEXAS.
2 MISS EMMA ARNALL, MAID OF HONOR.
3 MISS LOVE POUND,   "   "

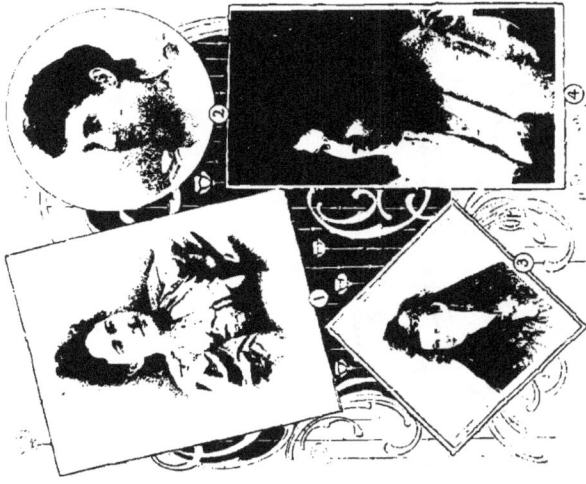

SANTOS BENEVIDES CAMP No. 637, LAREDO, TEXAS.

1 MISS MAY FOSTER, SPONSOR, LAREDO, TEXAS.
2 MISS EDNA TARVER, MAID OF HONOR.
3 MISS GEORGIE DODD,   "   "
4 MISS VIVA PENN.

MAGNOLIA CAMP, WOODVILLE, TEXAS.

1 MISS ADA SMITH, SPONSOR, WOODVILLE, TEXAS.
2 MISS BUELLEN GEISENDORF, MAID OF HONOR.

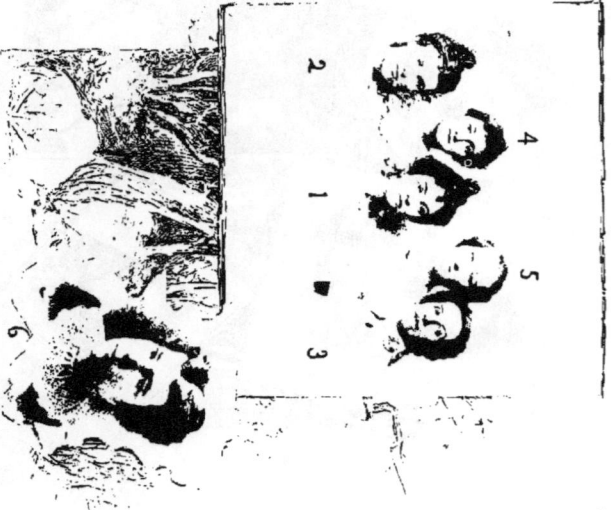

ROSS-ECTOR CAMP NO. 513, RUSK, TEXAS.

1 MISS HARRIETT CLAIBORNE, SPONSOR, RUSK, TEXAS.
2 MISS DODE NEELY, MAID OF HONOR.
3 MISS LENA RICKETTS, " "
4 MISS MAY BABONSFIELD, " "
5 MISS PHILD McCLURA, " "
6 MISS NETTIE REDWINE, " "

PROCTOR PORTER CAMP No. 608, WILLIS, TEXAS.

1 MISS PEARL SANDELL, SPONSOR, WILLIS, TEXAS.
2 MISS IONE BURNS, MAID OF HONOR.

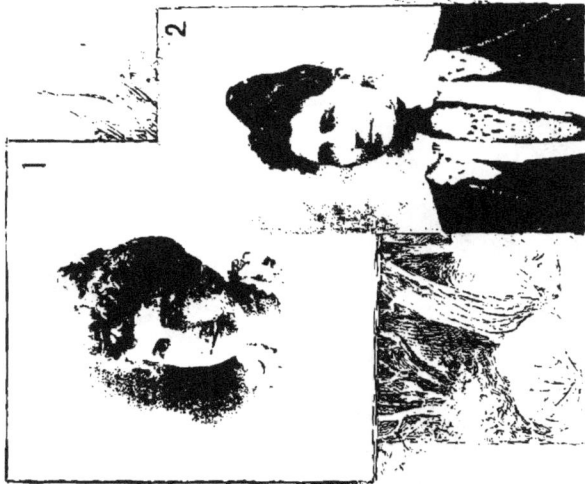

W. P. TOWNSEND CAMP No. 111, CALVERT, TEXAS.

1 MISS SUDIE HIGGS, SPONSOR, BREMOND, TEXAS.
2 MISS MINNIE EASTER, MAID OF HONOR.

SUL ROSS CAMP NO. 172, HENRIETTA, TEXAS.

1 MISS WILLIE A. J. PATTERSON, SPONSOR, HENRIETTA, TEXAS.
2 MISS WILLIE S. IKARD, MAID OF HONOR.

MILDRED LEE CAMP NO. 90, SHERMAN, TEXAS.

1 MISS MAY WILSON, SPONSOR, SHERMAN, TEXAS.
2 MISS BERNICE CARADINE, MAID OF HONOR.

RICHARD COKE CAMP NO. 600, ROBERT LEE, TEXAS.

2 MISS DONAH CRADDOCK, MAID OF HONOR.   1 MISS EMMA PAYNE, SPONSOR,   4 MISS SALLY PENNY, MAID OF HONOR.
3 MISS CORA SCARBOROUGH, "   "   SANCO, TEXAS.   5 MISS ARA CAMPBELL,   "   "

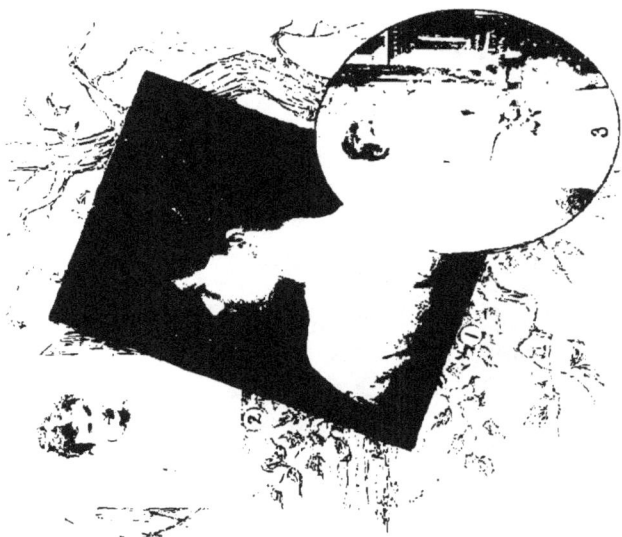

JOHN C. BROWN CAMP NO. 468, EL PASO, TEXAS.

1 MISS MARY C. BAYLOR, Sponsor, Eddy, New Mexico.
2 MISS LUCY KNELAND, Maid of Honor.
3 MISS MARY WHITE,   "   "

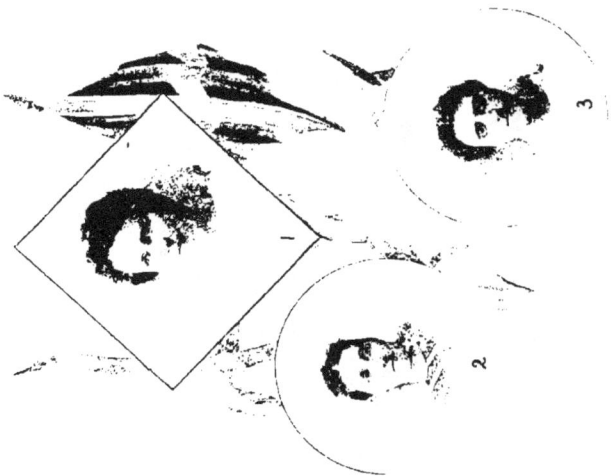

CLINTON TERRY CAMP, No. 245, BRAZORIA, TEXAS.

1 MISS ADDIE F. SMITH, Sponsor, Brazoria, Texas.
2 MISS BETTIE GUILD, Maid of Honor.
3 MRS. WHARTON BATES, Chaperon.

TOM GREEN CAMP NO. 136, HEMPSTEAD, TEXAS.

1 MISS BONNIE MILLS, Sponsor, Hempstead, Texas.
2 MISS MAGGIE E. THORNTON, Maid of Honor.
3 MISS STELLA SCHWARTZ, "
4 MRS. ELLA B. THORNTON, Chaperon.

E. B. PICKETT CAMP NO. 636, LIBERTY, TEXAS.

1 MISS ELIZA DEBLANC, Sponsor, Liberty, Texas.
2 MISS LEELA DEBLANC, Maid of Honor.
3 MISS WILDA D. WILLIAMS, "
4 MISS LEELA LUM, "

W. P. HARDEMAN CAMP NO. 604, YOAKUM, TEXAS.

1 MISS SUSIE L. EAVES, Sponsor, Yoakum, Texas.
2 Miss Ree Shropshire, Maid of Honor.
3 Miss Nannie Louie, " "

BUCHEL CAMP NO. 228, WHARTON, TEXAS.

1 MISS SUSIE DAMON, Sponsor, Wharton, Texas.
2 Miss Maggie Moore, Maid of Honor.
3 Miss Nannie Dennis, " "

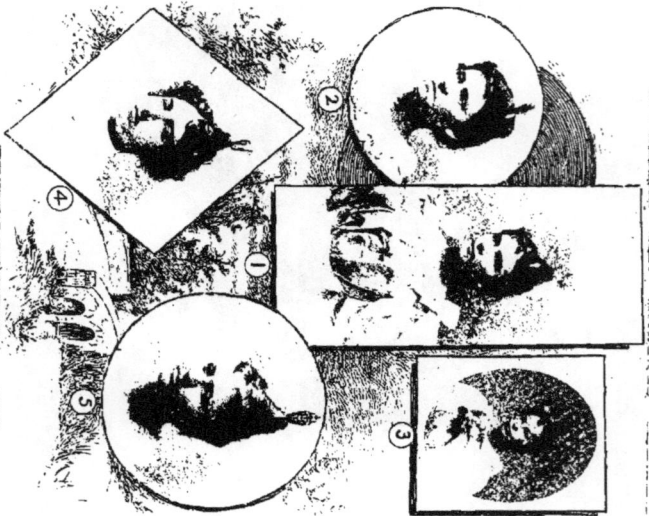

R. E. LEE CAMP NO. 66, LAMPASAS, TEXAS.

1 MISS BESSIE ANDREWS, SPONSOR, LAMPASAS, TEXAS.
2 MISS JESSIE WILLIAMSON, MAID OF HONOR.
3 MISS MAY ABNEY,   "   "   "
4 MISS MAUD SIMMONS,   "   "   "
5 MISS NOLIE THOMAS,   "   "   "

J. B. ROBINSON CAMP NO. 124, BRYAN, TEXAS.

1 MISS DAISY MONTGOMERY, SPONSOR, BRYAN, TEXAS.
2 MISS IVY CARNES, MAID OF HONOR.
3 MISS M. STELLA SHEPARD, MAID OF HONOR.

MISS BESSIE KENDALL, MAID OF HONOR.

Miss Mary Nevada Foscue, Maid of Honor.

Miss Mary F. Miller, Maid of Honor.

Miss Mary Agnes Henderson,
SULPHUR SPRINGS, TEXAS.
Sponsor, Camp Matt Ashcroft, No. 170.

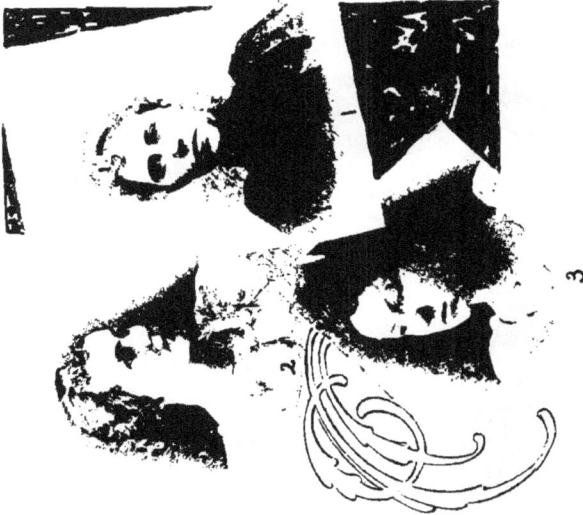

SAN FELIPE CAMP No. 624, SEALV, TEXAS.

1 MISS PEARL BOSTICK, Sponsor, Sealv, Texas.   1 MISS MAUD BUSHWALL, Sponsor, Sealv, Texas.
2 MISS EMMA HOWARD, Maid of Honor.   2 MISS JENNIE VICK, Maid of Honor.
3 MISS MAMIE COOK,   ''

KERRVILLE CAMP, KERRVILLE, TEXAS.

1 MISS ZORA MARTIN, SPONSOR,   7 MISS ANNA LOUISE BURNETT, MAID OF HONOR.
                KERRVILLE, TEXAS.   8 MISS EMMA NORWOOD,   "   "   "
5 MISS BUENA VISTA WILLIAMS, MAID OF HONOR. 9 MISS BETTIE BARTON, "   "   "
6 MISS LESA S. STEELE.

2 MISS DALLAS LOVE, MAID OF HONOR.
3 MISS MAGGIE VACN,   "   "   "
4 MISS ETTA LOWRY,   "   "   "

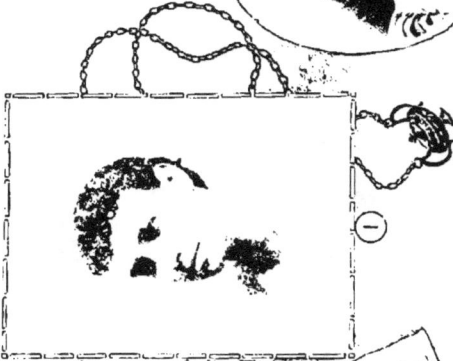

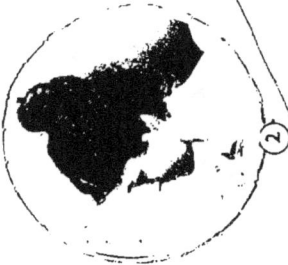

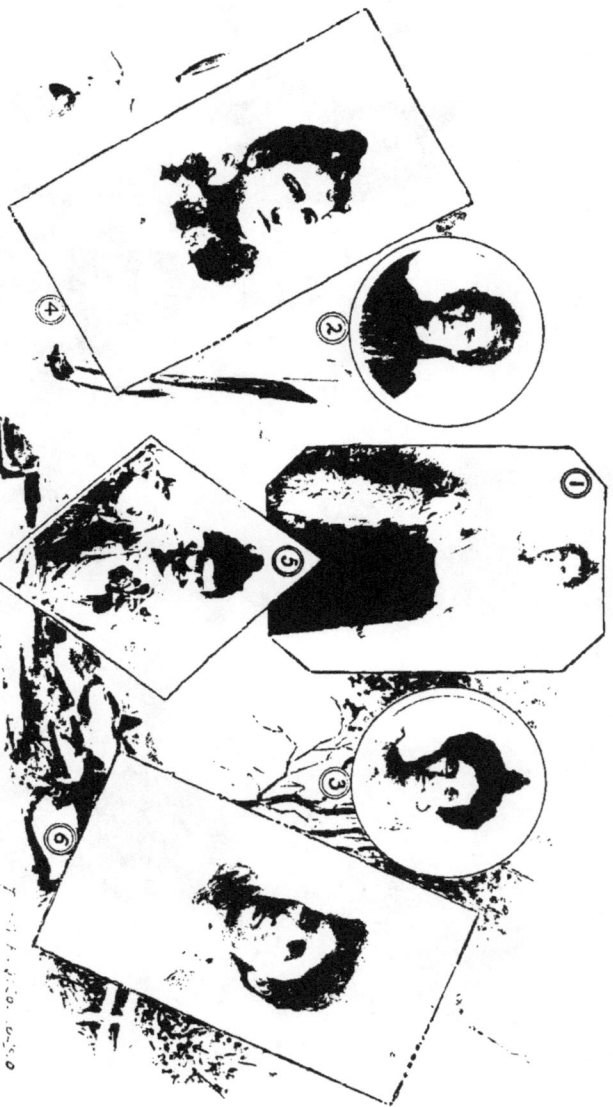

BEN McCULLOCH CAMP No. 29, CAMERON, TEXAS.

MISS LETTIE MO KEMP, Sponsor,
CAMERON, TEXAS.

2 MISS CLAUDIA TRACY, Maid of Honor.
3 MISS OZELLE RANDLE,   "
4 MISS MAE PERRY,   "

5 MISS DALLIE McIVER, Maid of Honor.
6 MISS NETTIE MOORE,   "

LLOYD TILGHMAN CAMP No. 463, PADUCAH, TEXAS.

1 MISS MIRIAM E. WHEELER, Sponsor, Richmond, Texas.

2 MISS ELLA MAE JORDAN, Maid of Honor.
3 MISS ANNIE JORDAN, "
4 MISS ISA M. COLLIER, "

5 MISS MAMIE J. THORNTON, Maid of Honor.
6 MISS MATTIE GERALDINE CRAIN, " "

WILLS POINT CAMP No. 302, WILLS POINT, TEXAS.

1 MISS NANNIE LUCINE PEASE, SPONSOR, WILLS POINT, TEXAS.

2 MISS MARTHA C. FORSYTH, MAID OF HONOR.
3 MISS NORA KEARBY, " "
4 MISS MYRTIE DEAN, " "

5 MISS LOUISA GORWYN, MAID OF HONOR.
6 MISS JOSIE ROBERTS, " "

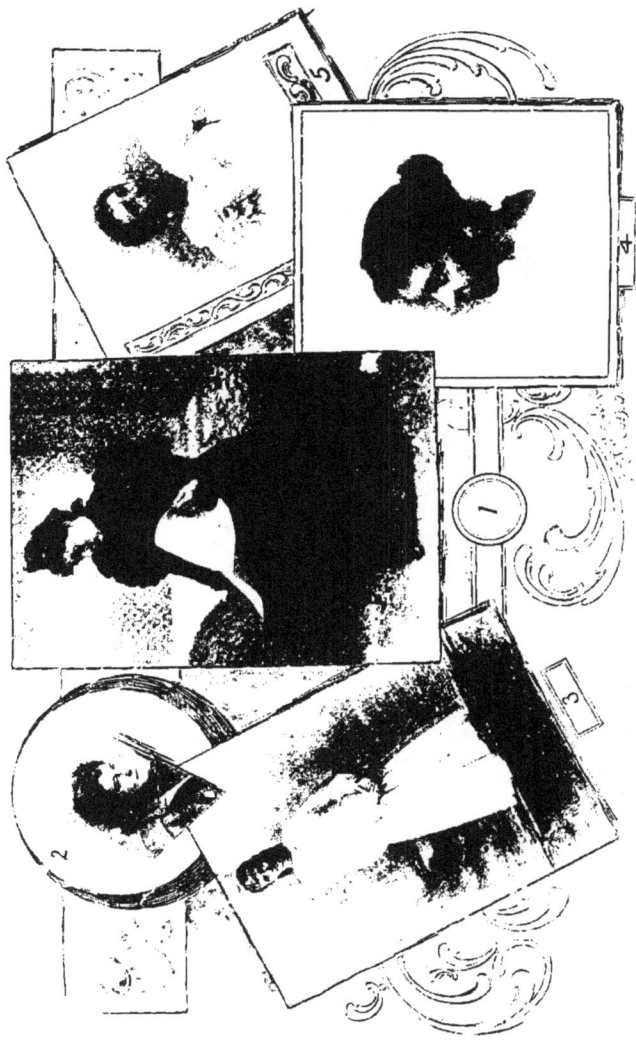

W. J. Hardee Camp No. 73, Wichita Falls, Texas.

2 Miss Avon McMurtry, Maid of Honor. 1 Miss Hallie Belle Crockett, Sponsor. 4 Miss Estelle Giddings, Maid of Honor.
3 Miss Katie Aylmer Word, " " 5 Miss Eula M. McCauley, "
Wichita Falls, Texas.

J. Warren Grigsby Camp No. 214, Houston, Texas.

1 Miss Nellie K. Shepherd, Sponsor, Houston, Texas.
2 Miss Blanche Dennis, Maid of Honor.
3 Miss Pierre Rushmore, "
4 Miss Aline Valerie Knight, Maid of Honor.
5 Miss Cora Shepherd, "

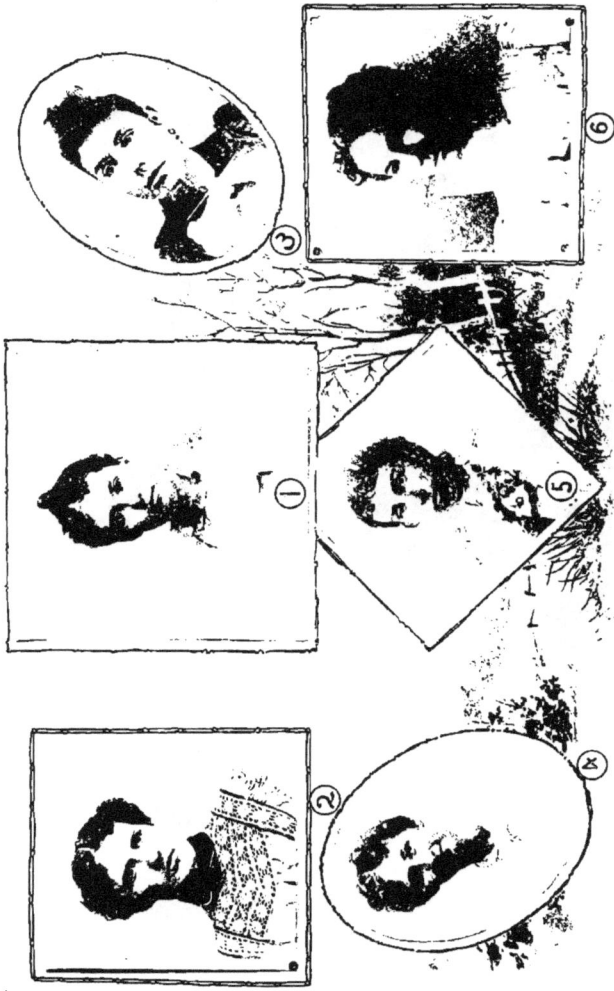

BELL COUNTY EX-CONFEDERATE ASSOCIATION CAMP No. 122, BELTON, TEXAS.

2 MISS JOSEPHINE DENISON, MAID OF HONOR. 1 MISS MINNIE BOYD, SPONSOR, 5 MISS DAISY TALLEY, MAID OF HONOR.
3 MISS ROBIS COX,   "   "   BELTON, TEXAS.   6 MISS MYRTLE PENDLETON, "   "
4 MISS LENA LOVE,   "   "

A. S. JOHNSTON CAMP No. 75, BEAUMONT, TEXAS.

1 MISS SADIE CASWELL, SPONSOR,
BEAUMONT, TEXAS.

2 MISS ALLIE O'BRIEN,   MAID OF HONOR.
3 MISS VIVA H. RUSSELL,   "   "
4 MISS ICY L. KONE,   "   "

5 MISS LILLIAN MYRICK,   MAID OF HONOR.
6 MISS NETTIE EASTHAM,   "   "
7 MISS VALLIE FLETCHER,   "   "

BEN MCCULLOUGH CAMP NO. 563, BRADY, TEXAS.

1 MISS ANNIE OGDEN, SPONSOR, BRADY, TEXAS.
2 MISS CLARA L. BALLOU, MAID OF HONOR.
3 MISS SALLIE JONES,   "   "

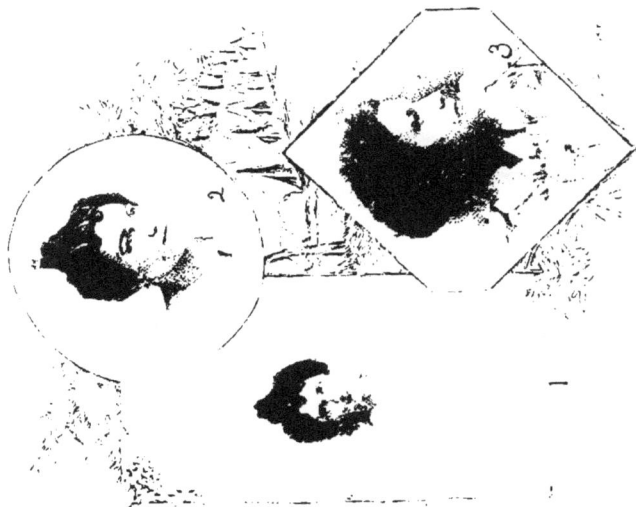

P. C. WOODS CAMP NO. 609, SAN MARCOS, TEXAS.

1 MISS PEARL HARDY, SPONSOR, SAN MARCOS, TEXAS.
2 MISS MAE TALBOT,   MAID OF HONOR.
3 MISS KATIE L. PACE,   "   "

SCHUYLER SUTTON CAMP NO. 605, SAN ANGELO, TEXAS.

1 MISS EVA MAGRUDER, SPONSOR, SAN ANGELO, TEXAS.
2 MISS MAMIE LEE, MAID OF HONOR.
3 MISS FLORENCE BROOME, " "

WILLIAM R. SCURRY CAMP NO. 516, VICTORIA, TEXAS.

1 MISS ETHEL B. BROWNSON, SPONSOR, VICTORIA, TEXAS.
2 MISS MILDRED FENNER, MAID OF HONOR.
3 MISS MILDRED L. AUSTIN, " "

GENERAL HOOD CAMP NO. 280, RIPLEY, TEXAS.

1 MISS MINNIE H. HOOD, SPONSOR, RIPLEY, TEXAS.
2 MISS JENNIE ROBERTSON, MAID OF HONOR,
3 MISS ANNA MARSHALL, " "
4 MISS LOU H. HOOD, " "

STONEWALL JACKSON CAMP NO. 118, BROWNWOOD, TEXAS.

1 MISS JOSEPHINE B. CABANISS, SPONSOR, BROWNWOOD, TEXAS.
2 MISS WILLIE CARTER, MAID OF HONOR,
3 MISS MOLLIE SMITH, " "
4 MISS RUTH TANNEHILL, " "

W. P. ROGERS CAMP No. 322, SAN SABA, TEXAS.

1 MISS CORDELIA OLIVER, SPONSOR, SAN SABA, TEXAS.
2 MISS EDNA OLIVER, MAID OF HONOR.

JEFF. DAVIS CAMP No. 386, SAN AUGUSTINE, TEXAS.

1 MISS ENNIE B. CALDWELL, SPONSOR, SAN AUGUSTINE, TEXAS.
2 MISS LOVONIA JOHNSON, MAID OF HONOR.

MISS FLEDA WYNNE.
PARIS, TEXAS.
Sponsor, A. S. Johnston Camp No. 70.

CLARA BELLE CHURCH.
OAKVILLE, TEXAS.
Sponsor, Jno. Donaldson Camp No. 195.

MRS. MATTIE WOOLERY.
CADDO MILLS, TEXAS.
Sponsor, Caddo Mills Camp No. 502.

Miss Emma T. Lemmon,
Trenton, Texas.
Sponsor, Camp John S. Bowen.

Miss Rozelle Nicholson,
Gouzales, Texas.
Sponsor, J. C. G. Key Camp, No. 156.

Miss Rachel D. Fraucks,
Marlin, Texas.
Sponsor, Willis Lang Camp No. 299.

MISS MARY HOLLAMON.
TAYLOR, TEXAS.
Sponsor, A. S. Johnston Camp No. 165.

MISS NELLIE D. KELLIE.
JASPER, TEXAS.
Sponsor, Camp J. E. Johnston.

MISS BERTIE KELLIE, MAID OF HONOR
TO MISS NELLIE KELLIE.

MISS MAUD NUNN, MAID OF HONOR.　　MISS LUCILE CHENOWETH NUNN.

MISS PEARL REVELL, MAID OF HONOR. MISS ELIZABETH STEGER, MAID OF HONOR.

SULL ROSS CAMP NO. 164, BONHAM, TEXAS.
Miss Lucile Chenoweth Nunn, Sponsor.

J. E. JOHNSTON CAMP No. 63, CORPUS CHRISTI, TEXAS.

2 MISS SEWALL CULPEPER,   MAID OF HONOR.   1 MISS ROXIE HASSELL, SPONSOR,   4 MISS TASSIE SPANN, MAID OF HONOR.
3 MISS ELIZABETH M. DOWNEY, "   "   CORPUS CHRISTI, TEXAS.

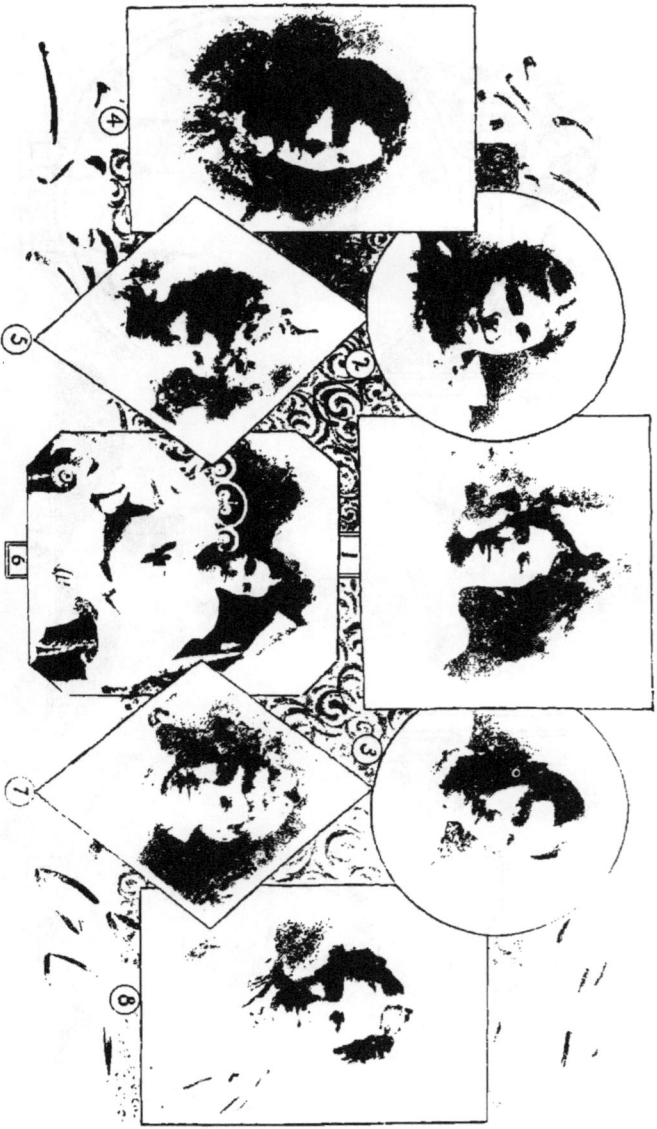

PIERCE B. ANDERSON CAMP No. 173, TULLAHOMA, TEXAS.

1 MISS FLORENCE WILSON, SPONSOR,
        TULLAHOMA, TEXAS.
5 MISS MARY LOU COWAN, MAID OF HONOR.

2 MISS FLORA V. ANDERSON, MAID OF HONOR.
3 MISS JESSIE MAI AYDELOTT, "
4 MISS MINNIE KINSEY, "

6 MISS CARRIE McLEMORE, MAID OF HONOR.
7 MISS EVA TRAVIS, "
8 MISS LOTTIE MARSHALL, "

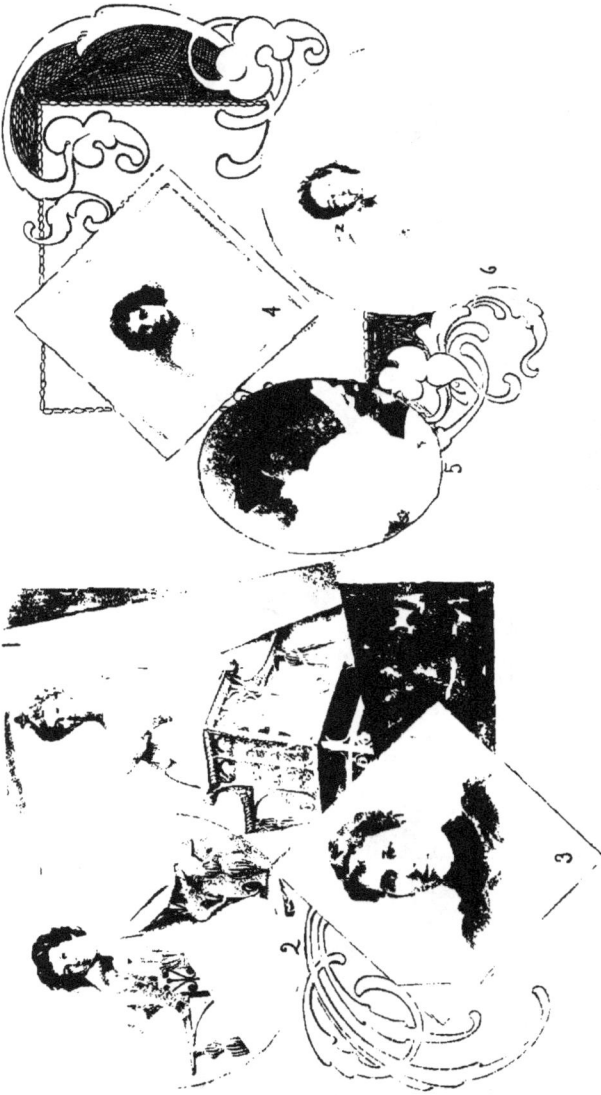

I. G. KILLOUGH CAMP NO. 593, FLATONIA, TEXAS.

1 MISS SUSIE LANE, SPONSOR,
FLATONIA, TEXAS,

2 MISS FANNIE LANE, JR., MAID OF HONOR.
3 MISS LELA CADWELL, "   "
4 MISS EDNA SULLIVAN, "   "

5 MISS TILLIE STOFFUS, MAID OF HONOR.
6 MISS MAYNIE CADWELL, "   "

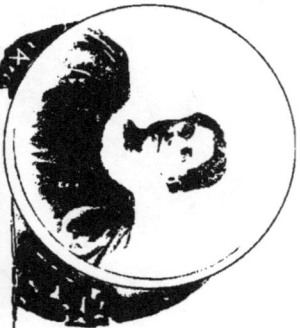

A. S. JOHNSTON CAMP NO. 116, HAMILTON, TEXAS.

2 MISS ANNIE PECK, MAID OF HONOR.
3 MISS MEDA GENEVRA SPARKMAN, MAID OF HONOR.
4 MISS BESSIE SAXON, SPONSOR, HAMILTON, TEXAS.
1 MISS MAGGIE AVENT, MAID OF HONOR.
5 MRS. ADA HOOKS, CHAPERON.

COLONEL B. TIMMONS CAMP No. 61, LaGRANGE, TEXAS.

1 MISS LEE KILLOUGH, Sponsor, LaGrange, Texas.
2 MISS MAMIE TROUSDALE, Maid of Honor.
3 MISS EMMA MAY O'HAR,   "   "
4 MISS TUMMIE FAINES,   "   "

IKE TURNER CAMP No. 321, MOSCOW, TEXAS.

1 MISS OLIVE E. TACKABERRY, Sponsor, Moscow, Texas.
2 MISS BONNIE TACKABERRY, Maid of Honor.
3 MISS MARY POE,   "   "
4 MISS NETTIE CANON,   "   "

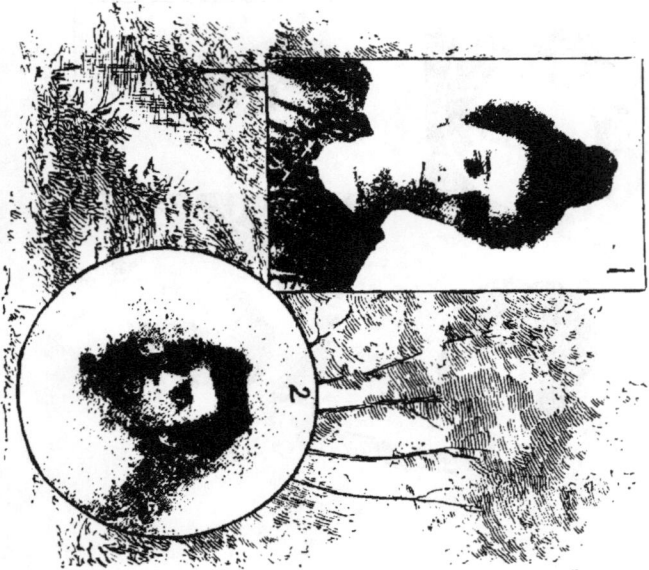

GEORGE E. PICKETT CAMP No. 570, LOCKHART, TEXAS.

1 MISS ESTELLE L. STOREY, SPONSOR, AUSTIN, TEXAS.
2 MISS E. B. MYERS, MAID OF HONOR.

JOHN A. WHARTON CAMP No. 286, ALVIN, TEXAS.

1 MISS MARY ROGERS, SPONSOR, ALVIN, TEXAS.
2 MISS BLANCHE PARKER, MAID OF HONOR.
3 MISS JOSIE SMITH, "   "

E. KIRBY SMITH CAMP NO. 251, WACO, TEXAS.

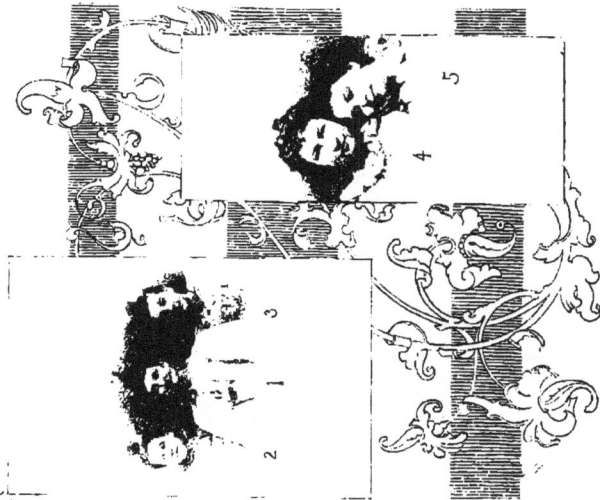

JOHN PELHAM CAMP NO. 76, COLEMAN, TEXAS.

BEDFORD FOREST CAMP No. 86, SEYMOUR, TEXAS.

1 MISS BIRDIE MAY COOPER, SPONSOR, SEYMOUR, TEXAS.
2 MISS IRENE BRANHAM, MAID OF HONOR, SEYMOUR, TEXAS.

J. E. B. STUART CAMP No. 45, TERRELL, TEXAS.

1 MISS ANNYE G. NEBHUT, SPONSOR, TERRELL, TEXAS.
2 MISS EVA BOND, MAID OF HONOR.

WALTON CAMP NO. 575, BEEVILLE, TEXAS.

1 MISS NORINE WALTON, SPONSOR, BEEVILLE, TEXAS.
2 MISS PEARL R. ATKINS, MAID OF HONOR.
3 MISS NELLIE ARCHER, " "

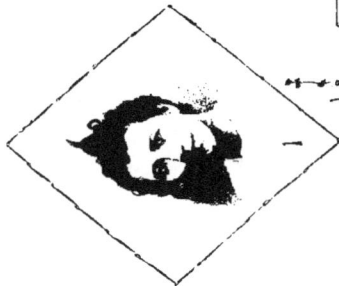

JEFF. DAVIS CAMP NO. 117, GOLDTHWAITE, TEXAS.

1 MISS HELEN SIMMS, SPONSOR, SULPHUR SPRINGS, TEXAS.
2 MISS DORA HUMPHRIES, MAID OF HONOR.
3 MRS. HUMPHRIES, CHAPERON.

ALBERT SIDNEY JOHNSTON CAMP No. 48, TYLER, TEXAS.

1 MISS MITTIE MARSH, Sponsor, Tyler, Texas.
2 MISS LELA ROBERTSON, Maid of Honor.
3 MISS NETTIE BAKER, "

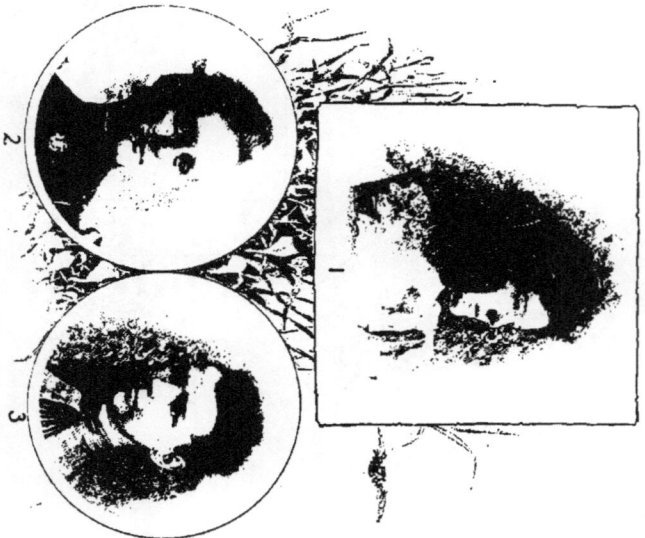

ROGER W. HUSSON CAMP No. 186, HOUSTON, TEXAS.

1 MISS HATTIE F. SMITH, Sponsor, Houston, Texas.
2 MISS LUCY C. SMITH, Maid of Honor.
3 MISS SUSIE FRASHAKE, "

H. G. LANE CAMP No. 614, LUFKIN, TEXAS.

6 MISS DAISY WARREN, SPONSOR.

1 MISS NANNIE McMASTER, MAID OF HONOR,   4 MISS LILLIE McMULLEN, MAID OF HONOR.
2 MISS LUCY YOUNG,   "   "   5 MISS JANIE WARREN,   "   "
3 MISS AUGUSTA WILSON,   "   "   7 MISS ADDIE HANDLEY,   "   "

MISS MARY R. TURNER, MAID OF HONOR

TO MISS A. W. TURNEY.

MISS ANNIE W. TURNEY.

TEXARKANA, TEXAS.

Sponsor, A. P. Hill Camp No. 269.

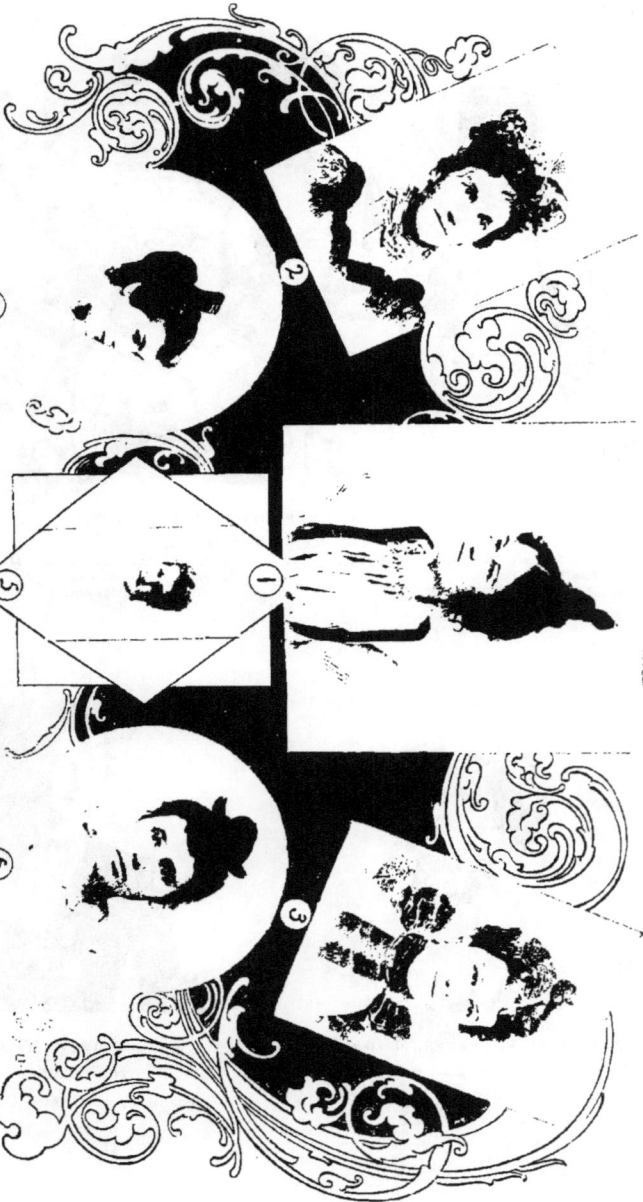

JOHN C. UPTON CAMP No. 43, HUNTSVILLE, TEXAS.

1 MISS ROBBIE BUSH, SPONSOR, HUNTSVILLE, TEXAS.

2 MISS MAGGIE WOODALL, MAID OF HONOR.
4 MISS IDA ANGIER, " "
5 MISS MAE ANGIER, " "

6 MISS LETTIE BRANCH, MAID OF HONOR.
7 MRS. JULIETTE BUSH, CHAPERON.

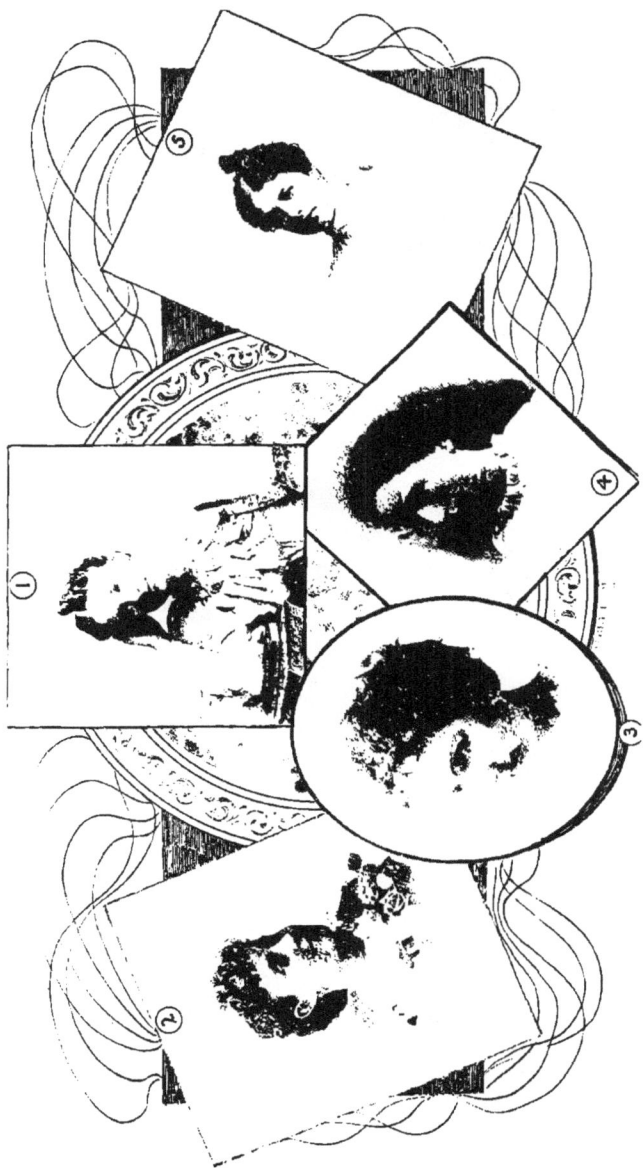

DICK DOWLING CAMP No. 197, HOUSTON, TEXAS.

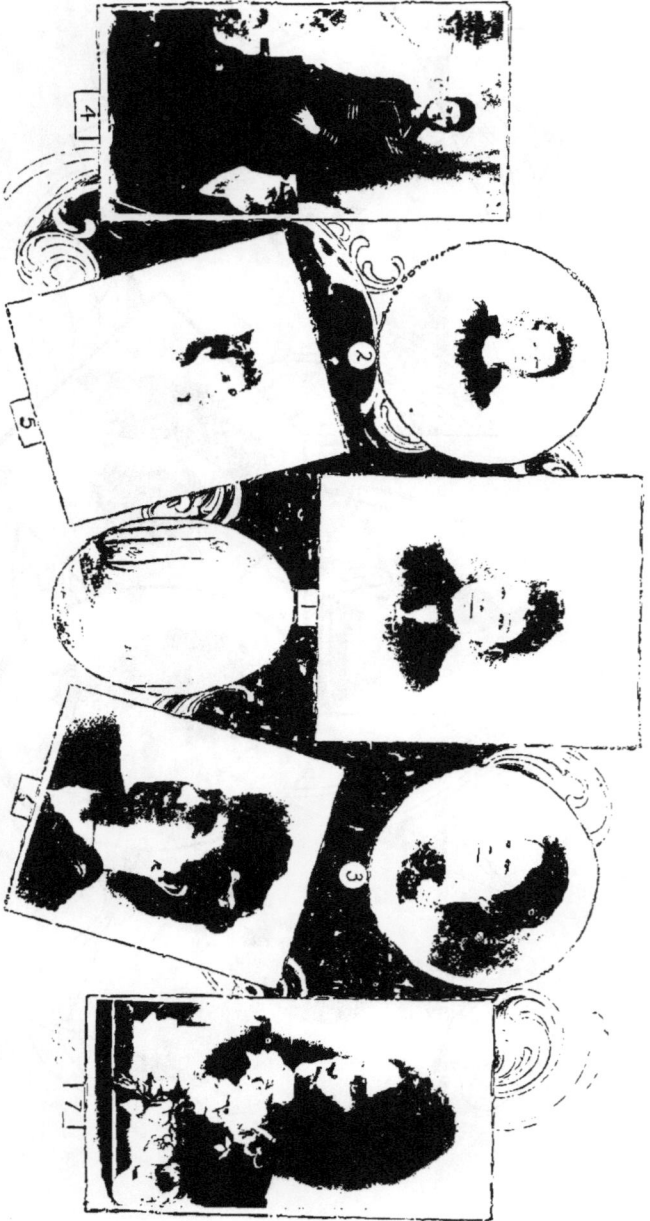

L. F. MOODY CAMP NO. 123, BUFFALO GAP, TEXAS.

1 MISS BANIE LYON, SPONSOR,
BUFFALO GAP, TEXAS.

2 MISS ROZELLE EUBANK, MAID OF HONOR,
3 MISS LELA MAI HICKMAN, "   "
4 MISS BEULAH SPRINGFIELD, "   "

5 MISS MATTIE MCCUISON, MAID OF HONOR,
6 MISS VILLA CAXON,   "   "
7 MISS WILLIE NEAL,   "   "

VELOSCO CAMP NO. 592, VELOSCO, TEXAS.

2 MISS EULA GEE, SPONSOR, VELOSCO, TEXAS.
1 MISS ANNA TROTTER, MAID OF HONOR.
3 MISS HIGHLAND GEE, " "

JOHN W. CALDWELL CAMP NO. 139, RUSSELLVILLE, KENTUCKY.

1 MISS ANNIE SOMERVILLE, SPONSOR, RICHMOND, TEXAS.
2 MISS ELLA B. SOMERVILLE, MAID OF HONOR.
3 MISS VINNIE FERRIS, " "
4 MISS NELLIE FERRIS, " "

MAIDS OF HONOR TO MISS JOVITA BOYD.

1 Miss Bonnie Dunlavy.
1 Miss Lucy Belle Mitchell.
, Miss Mamie Davis.
, Miss Hattie Jones.

Miss Jovita Boyd,
RICHMOND, TEXAS.
State Sponsor for Kentucky Division.

THOS. B. MONROE CAMP NO. 188, FRANKFORT, KY.

1 MISS EVA V. ALLEN, SPONSOR, WACO, TEXAS.
2 MISS ETHEL OLIPHINT, MAID OF HONOR.
3 MISS GENIE MOON,   "   "
4 MISS SUDIE DAVIS,   "   "
5 MISS GRACE BURKE,   "   "

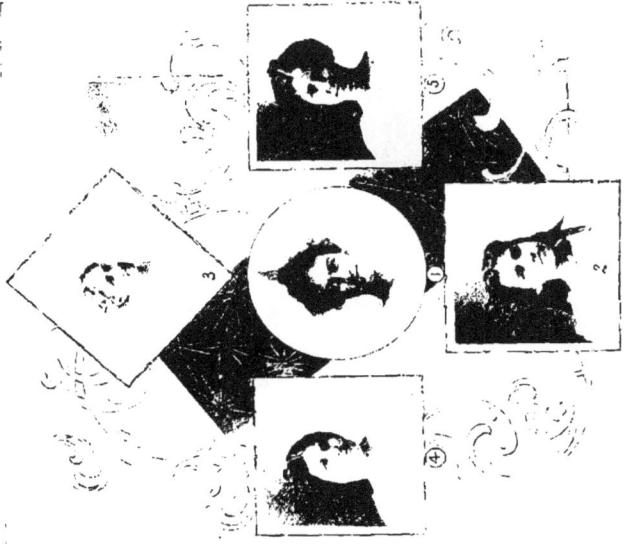

JOHN C. BRECKENRIDGE CAMP NO. 100, LEXINGTON, KY.

1 MISS ALETHA NEAL, SPONSOR, RICHMOND, TEXAS.
2 MISS ETHEL PEARSON, MAID OF HONOR.
3 MISS WILLEN GROCE,   "   "
4 MISS WINNIE McGEE,   "   "

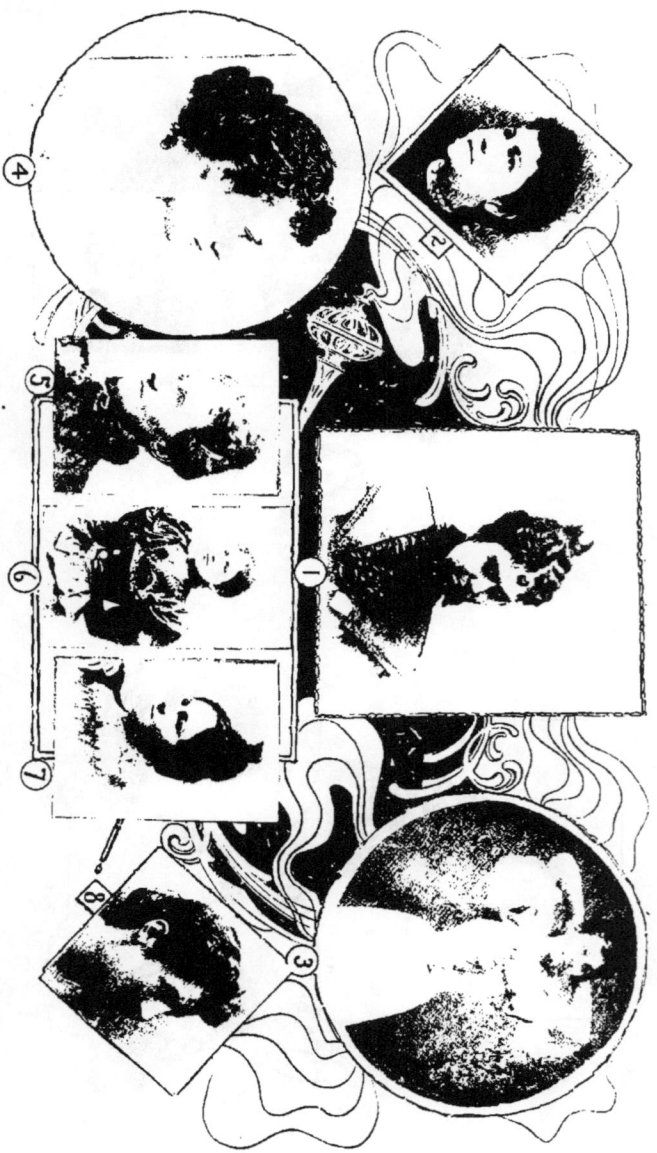

HON. POLK LAFFOON CAMP NO. 528, MADISONVILLE, KY.

1 MISS EMMA LAFFOON, SPONSOR,   6 MISS MATTIE V. BROOKS, MAID OF HONOR.
   MADISONVILLE, KY.   7 MRS. GEORGIA COMPTON,   "   "
5 MISS C. F. HOCKERSMITH, MAID OF HONOR.   8 MRS. FANNIE BOURBARD,   "   "

2 MISS EMMA STEVENS, MAID OF HONOR.
3 MISS LULA HARDMAN,   "   "
4 MISS MOLLIE WINGO,   "   "

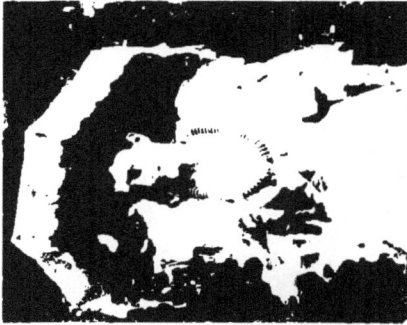

Miss Margaret L. Banks.

Sponsor, Horace King Camp No. 476,
Decatur, Ala.

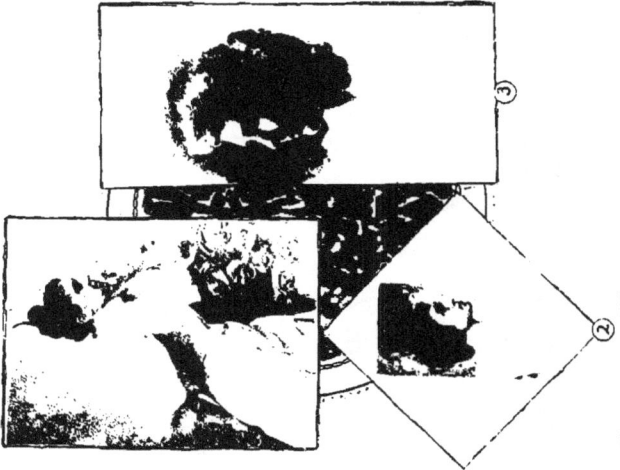

George W. Johnson Camp No. 98, Georgetown, Ky.

1 Miss Mary Bell Halley, Sponsor, Paynes Depot, Ky.
2 Miss Julia Halley,   Maid of Honor.
3 Miss Sydney Scott Lewis,   "

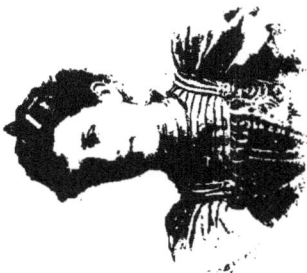

Miss Lillie May Hollingsworth,
sponsor,
Confederate Veterans Camp No. 527,
Princeton, Ky.

MISS MARY HARALSON,
MONTGOMERY, ALA.
MAID OF HONOR TO MISS ELLA NELSON.

MISS ELLA NELSON,
SELMA, ALA.
State Sponsor for Alabama.

AIKIN SMITH CAMP NO. 293, ROANOKE, ALA.

1 MISS EFFIE WEATHERS, SPONSOR, ROANOKE, ALA.
2 MISS ELLA CARLISLE, MAID OF HONOR.
3 MISS ARRIE HUDSON, "
4 MISS NORA WRIGHT, "
5 MISS SALLIE DRIVER, MAID OF HONOR.
6 MISS SUSIE CARLISLE, MAID OF HONOR.
7 MISS LENA USSERY, "
8 MISS TILMOE MOON, "

CAMP FORCE NO. 459, BROOKWOOD, ALA.

1   MISS LENA KOEPPEL, SPONSOR.   4   MISS LOLA R. BEATTY, MAID OF HONOR.
        COALING, ALA.

2   MISS LOLA CURRY, MAID OF HONOR.
3   MISS LILLA NELSON, "

FRANKLIN K. BECK CAMP No. 224, CAMDEN, ALA.

2 MISS KATE C. GAILLARD, MAID OF HONOR.   1 MISS EMMIE D. MOORE, SPONSOR.   6 MISS ANNIE MAY JONES,   MAID OF HONOR.
3 MISS FANNIE W. PURIFOY,   "   CAMDEN, ALA.   7 MISS ANNIE ERVIN MCWILLIAMS,   "
4 MISS WILLIE E. DEXTER,   "   "   5 MISS EMMIE L. MCNEILL, MAID OF HONOR.   8 MISS KATIE R. JONES,   "

R. H. G. GAINES CAMP NO. 370, LOWER PEACH TREE, ALA.

1 MISS ANNIE PACKER WELSH, SPONSOR, LOWER PEACH TREE, ALA.

2 MISS MARTHA STABLER, MAID OF HONOR.
3 MISS FLORENCE IRBY,   "   "
4 MISS JULIA MAYER,   "   "

5 MISS JULIA POSTIS,   MAID OF HONOR.
6 MISS OLA McCONNELL,   "   "
7 MISS SADIE ROBINS,   "   "

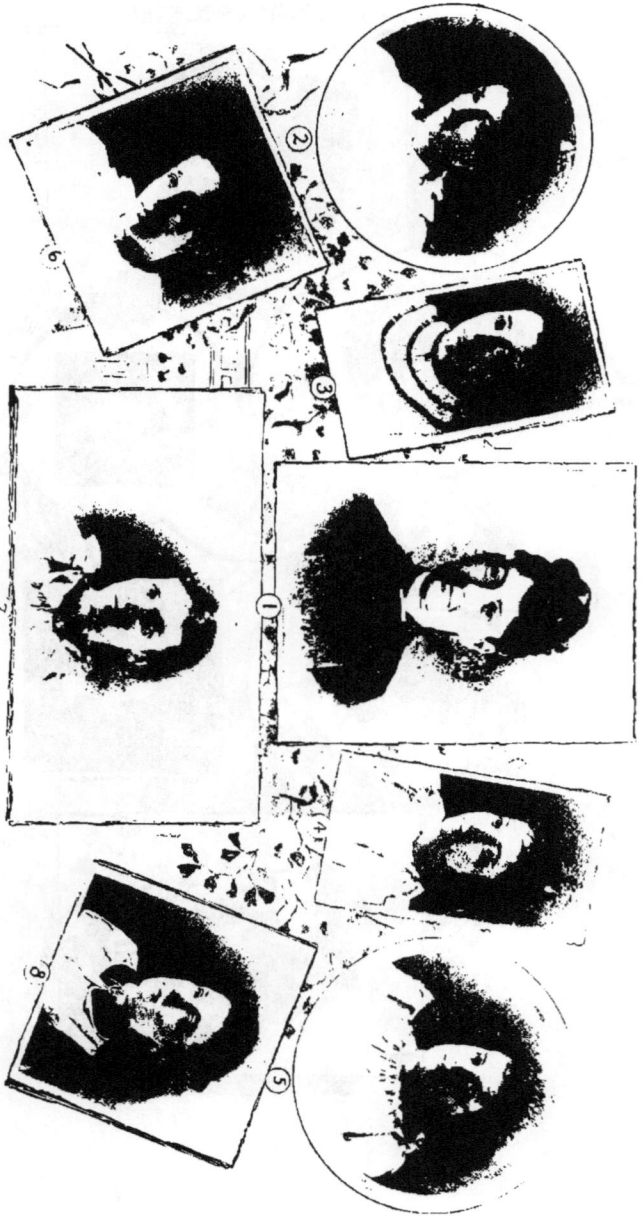

CRAWF. KIMBALL CAMP NO. 343, DADEVILLE, ALA.

1 MRS. JAMES JOHNSON, SPONSOR,
   DADEVILLE, ALA.
2 MISS MARY BELLE VINES, MAID OF HONOR.
3 MISS EMILY T. HERNEN,   "   "
4 MISS CLITIE BLOODWORTH,   "   "
5 MISS FANNIE E. BURGER, MAID OF HONOR.
6 MISS WILL ELLA McINTOSH, MAID OF HONOR.
7 MISS BESSIE ROWE,   "   "
8 MISS CORA BLACK,   "   "

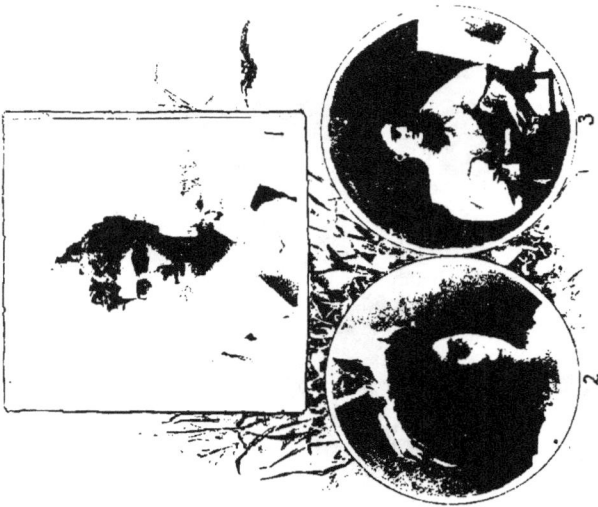

LEE CAMP No. 329.

1 MISS ESTER SMITH, Sponsor, Oxford, Ala.
2 Miss Manie Casey, Maid of Honor.
3 Miss Bettie Forbes, "   "   "
4 Miss Leilo Miller, "   "   "
5 Miss Nannie Smith, "   "   "

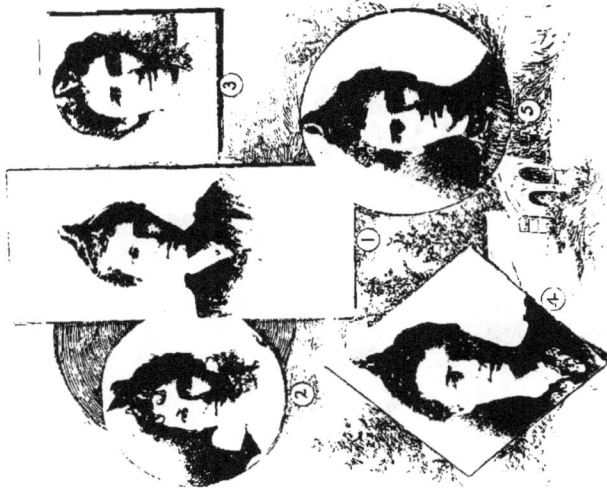

RHODES CAMP No. 262, TUSCALOOSA, ALA.

1 MISS ANNIE MAY OGBURN, Sponsor, Tuscaloosa, Ala.
2 Miss Annie Laurie Clements, Maid of Honor.
3 Miss Maude S. Howell, "   "   "

SANDERS CAMP NO. 64, EUTAW, ALA.

1   MISS FLORENCE C. REESE, SPONSOR, EUTAW, ALA.
2   MISS SARAH SHAW,   MAID OF HONOR.
3   MISS ADDIE M. SPENCER,   "   "

BESSEMER CAMP NO. 157, BESSEMER, ALA.

1   MISS AMY WELTON McADORY, SPONSOR, BESSEMER, ALA.
2   MISS NANNIE H. HOWELL, MAID OF HONOR.

MISS GERTRUDE JONES,
SPONSOR.

MISS LYLE OVERTON DAVIDSON,
MAID OF HONOR.

MISS MARY PAGE JONES.
MAID OF HONOR.

MISS LOUISE RENIER COMPTON,
MAID OF HONOR.

CAMP CATSBY A. R. JONES, SELMA, ALA.

MISS OLLIE LOU STANSEL,
SPONSOR,
CARROLLTON, ALA.

MISS FLORENCE DeLOACH,
MAID OF HONOR,
LIVINGSTON, ALA.

MISS AMY HUBBARD,
MAID OF HONOR,

MISS NETTIE MURPHREE,
MAID OF HONOR.

PICKENS CAMP NO. 323, CARROLLTON, ALA.

Miss Corinne Thibault.
New Orleans, La.
State Sponsor for Maryland.

Ridgely Brown Camp No. 518, Gaithersburgh, Maryland.

1 Miss Fannie L. Amiss, Sponsor, Gaithersburgh, Maryland.
2 Miss Mary E. Chiswell, Maid of Honor.
3 Miss Mattie Thomas,   "   "
4 Miss Lucy Rice,   "   "

STONEWALL JACKSON CAMP NO. 42, McKENZIE, TENN.

1 MISS FANNIE M. BAXTER, Sponsor, McKenzie, Tenn.
2 MISS OLA BARKSDALE, Maid of Honor, McKenzie, Tenn.
3 MISS MADGE CANNON,   "   "

MISS CARRIE MONTAGUE JENNINGS,
MT. PLEASANT, TENN.
State Sponsor for Tennessee.

F

MISS LIDA KELLY.

WINDSOR, MO.

State Sponsor for Missouri.

GEN. J. S. MARMADUKE CAMP NO. 554, MARSHALL, MO.

1 MISS ETHLYNE JACKSON, SPONSOR, MARSHALL, MO.
2 MISS KATE McMAHAN,   MAID OF HONOR.
3 MISS MINNIE I. TUCKER,   "   "
4 MISS BERTA LEE FRANCISCO,   "   "

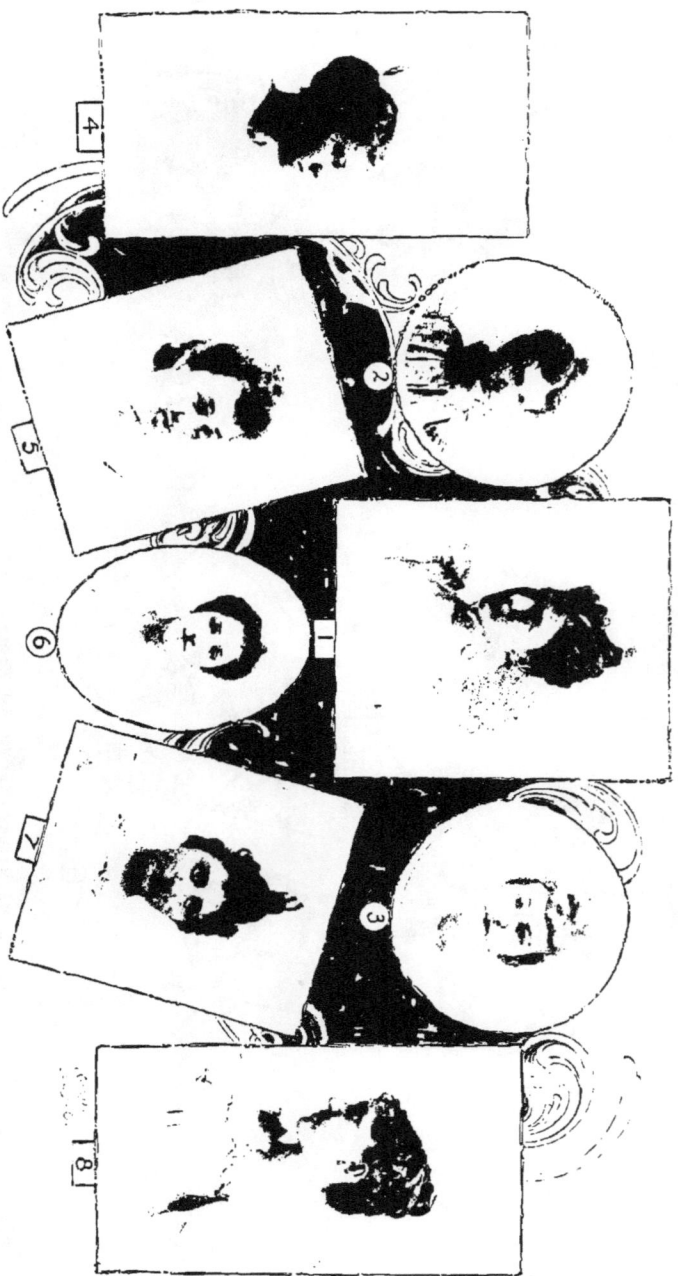

THOMAS G. LOWRY CAMP NO. 636, HUNTSVILLE, MO.

1 MISS MARY A. STUART, SPONSOR, HUNTSVILLE, MO.
2 MISS ALMA SELLERS, MAID OF HONOR.
3 MISS VALLIE RICHESON, "   "
4 MISS LOIS RATLIFF, "   "
5 MISS NANNIE HEFLIN, MAID OF HONOR.
6 MISS BLANCHE BUCHANAN, MAID OF HONOR.
7 MISS ANNIE MILLER, "   "
8 MISS LAURA V. BALTHIS, "   "

L. C. CAMPBELL CAMP No. 488, SPRINGFIELD, MO.

2 MISS MYRTLE HOGAN,   MAID OF HONOR.   1 MISS WINNIE HOGAN, SPONSOR,   5 MISS MATTIE CANTRELL, MAID OF HONOR.
3 MISS DORA ALICE WILSON,   "   "   SPRINGFIELD, MO.   6 MISS WILLIE HINTON,   "   "
4 MISS CLARA LABAREE GOFFE,   "   "

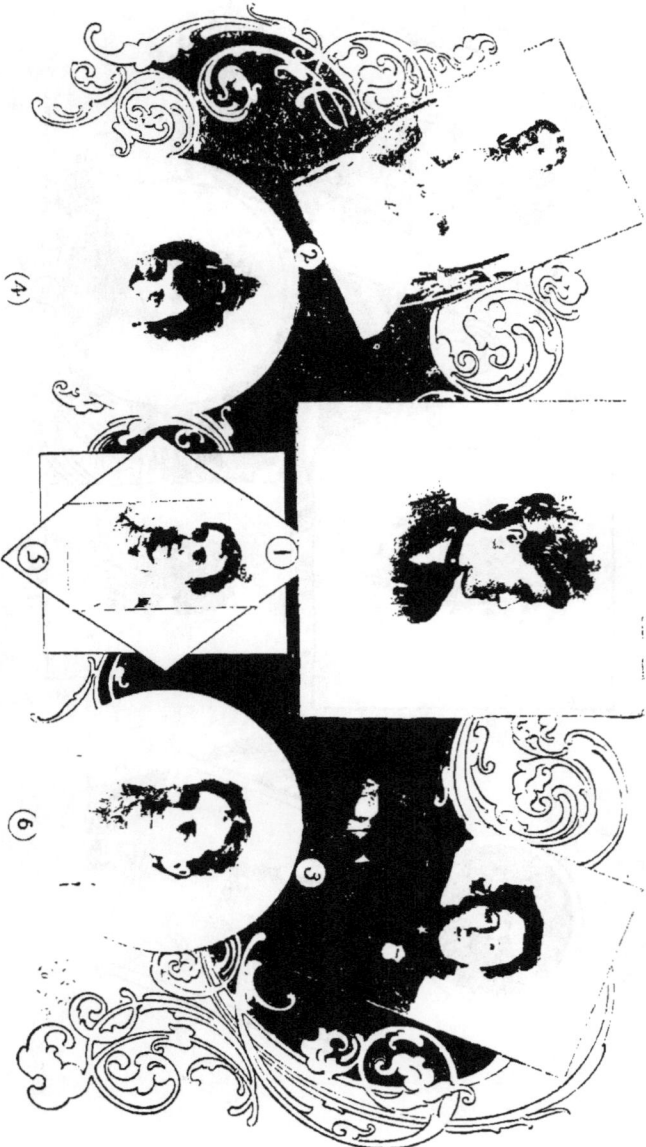

STERLING PRICE CAMP No. 547, ODESSA, Mo.

1 MISS IDA IRENE GUM, SPONSOR,
ODESSA, Mo.

2 MISS LILLIE FOX, MAID OF HONOR,
3 MISS LUCILE CHRISTIE, "   "
4 MISS EVALYN M. PARKER, "   "

5 MISS SUE M. GROSSHART, MAID OF HONOR,
6 MISS DORA ALICE LEE, "   "

MARMADUKE CAMP No. 615, BUTLER, MO.

2 MISS MARY LOTSPEICH,   MAID OF HONOR.   1 MISS ROBERTA CATRON. SPONSOR.   5 MISS LUCILE SEVIER, MAID OF HONOR.
3 MISS MARGARET MAE NICKELL, "   "   BUTLER, MO.   6 MISS OLIVE SIMPSON,   "   "
4 MISS MARELLE MARTIN,   "   "

CAPT. DAVID HAMMONS CAMP No. 177, OKLAHOMA CITY, OKLAHOMA TERRITORY.

1 MRS. LILLIE G. HARWOOD, MAID OF HONOR. 2 MRS. MARY A. RIPPLE, SPONSOR. 4 MISS JESSIE BAILY, MAID OF HONOR.
1 MISS LUCILLE B. CASLER, " " 3 MISS LUCILLE B. CASLER, " HUTCHINS, KANSAS.

CROFT CAMP NO. 530, ZACKARY, LA.

1 MISS MARY A. LEE, SPONSOR, ZACKARY, LA.
2 MISS LILLIAN LEE, MAID OF HONOR.

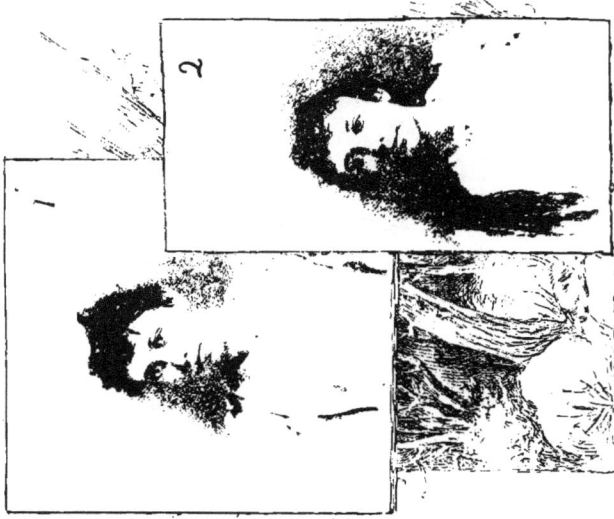

CALCASIEU CAMP NO. 62, LAKE CHARLES, LA.

1 MISS HATTIE L. READ, SPONSOR, LAKE CHARLES, LA.
2 MISS LUCIE GOODLETT, MAID OF HONOR.

HOOD CAMP NO. 589, LOGANSPORT, LA.

1 MISS BESSIE E. PRICE, SPONSOR, LOGANSPORT, LA.
2 MISS CORINNE MCMILLAN, MAID OF HONOR
3 MISS BETTIE NASH,   "   "
4 MISS MAMIE GARRETT,   "   "

DICK TAYLOR CAMP NO. 546, PLEASANT HILL, LA.

1 MISS MARY E. GRAHAM, SPONSOR, PLEASANT HILL, LA.
2 MISS MABEL HARREL, MAID OF HONOR.
3 MISS LOUISE HARREL,   "   "

BRAXTON BRAGG CAMP NO. 196, THIBODEAUX, LA.

1 MISS MAMIE C. WALSH, Sponsor,
      THIBODEAUX, LA.

2 MISS LIZZIE BEAUVAIS, MAID OF HONOR.
3 MISS EDNA J. TUCKER,   "
4 MISS CELESTE AUCOIN,   "

5 MISS SARAH JOSEPHINE GAGNE, MAID OF HONOR.
6 MISS ANNETTE COULON,   "

MISS ADA T. RICHARDSON.

NEW ORLEANS, LA.

State Sponsor for Virginia.

L. B. SMITH CAMP No. 402, TALBOTTON, GA.

1 MISS LYNDA L. LEE, Sponsor, Talbotton, Ga.
2 MISS JENNIE BEALL McCoy, Maid of Honor.
3 MISS LIZZIE V. CARTER,   "   "
4 MISS CLAUDIA BELL LEE,   "   "

MISS KATIE BRENT.
MAID OF HONOR
TO MISS CLARA CHIPLEY.

MISS CLARA CHIPLEY.
PENSACOLA, FLA.
State Sponsor for Florida.

FLORIDA LAKE CO. CONF. VET. ASS'N CAMP NO. 279, TAVARES, FLA.

1 MISS XENA DeWITT HERNDON, Sponsor, Leesburg, Fla.
2 MISS MABELL MILAM, Maid of Honor.

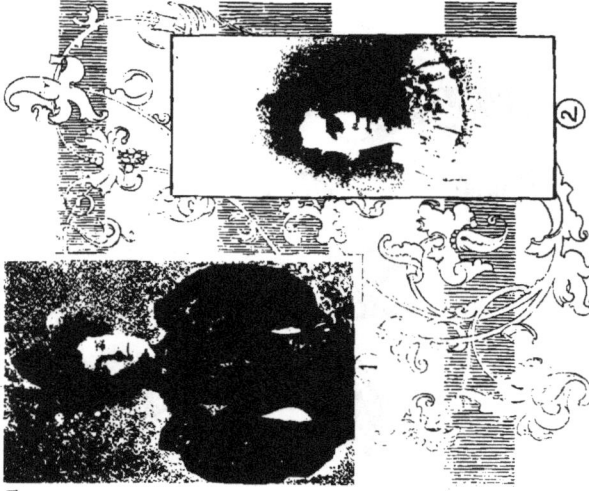

MARION COUNTY CONF. VETERANS CAMP NO. 56, OCALA, FLA.

1 MISS KATHARINE EUGENIA LIVINGSTON, Sponsor, Ocala, Fla.
2 MISS MARIE VANN DIAL, Maid of Honor.

D. L. KENAN CAMP NO. 140, QUINCY, FLA.

1 MISS ELLA LOVE, SPONSOR, QUINCY, FLA.
2 MISS NENIE MONROE, MAID OF HONOR.
3 MISS BESSIE LOVE, " "
4 MISS EMMIE WILSON, " "

E. A. PERRY CAMP NO. 150, WELBORN, FLA.

1 MISS LIZZIE A. MOORE, SPONSOR, WELBORN, FLA.
2 MISS CILLA GRIFFIN, MAID OF HONOR.
3 MISS RUBIE SCARBOROUGH, " "
4 MISS JESSIE IVES, " "

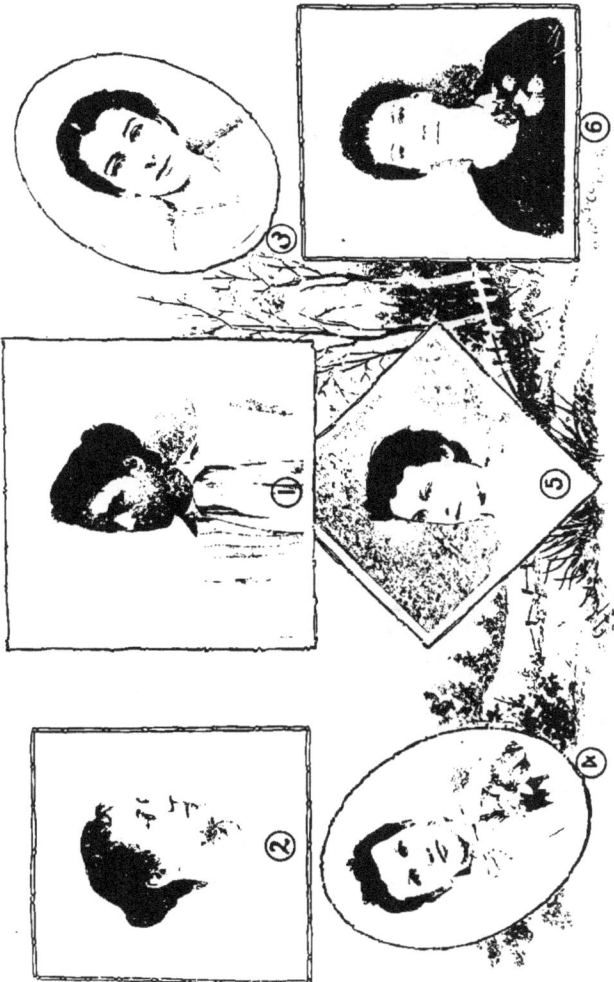

COBB CAMP NO. 538, MILTON, FLORIDA.

1 MISS LAURA BRASHEARS, SPONSOR,
MILTON, FLA.

2 MISS ISABELL HARRISON, MAID OF HONOR.
3 MISS MARY ELLIS, " "
4 MISS EDNA SEABROOK, " "
5 MISS MINNIE ALLEN, MAID OF HONOR.
6 MISS DERLIE FISHER, " "

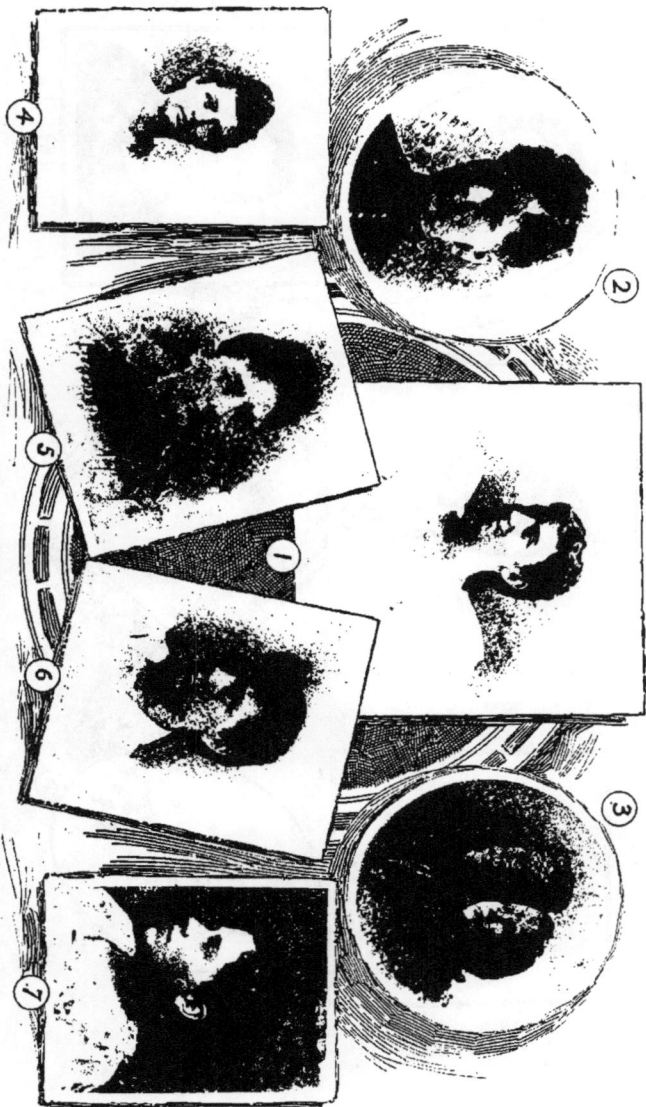

SAM COMMACK CAMP NO. 550, CLARKSDALE, MISS.

1   MISS KATIE RIVERS HARRIS, SPONSOR,
        CLARKSDALE, MISS.

2   MISS JOSIE ALLEN,   MAID OF HONOR.
3   MISS ELIZABETH DABNEY, "
4   MISS CLARA LEE ALCORN, "

5   MISS ELLIS,   MAID OF HONOR.
6   MISS FANNIE SIMMONS,   "
7   MISS FOUNTAINE,   "

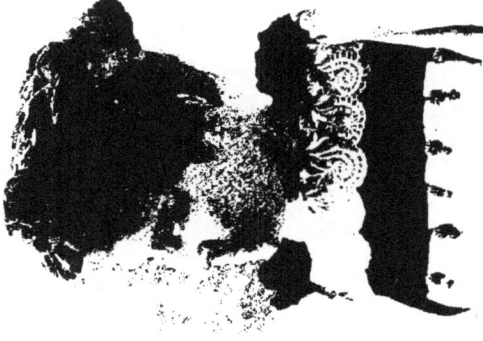

MISS LONLIE F. PRICE.

MAID OF HONOR

TO MISS LORENA McINTOSH.

MISS LORENA McINTOSH.

MERIDIAN, MISS.

State Sponsor for Mississippi.

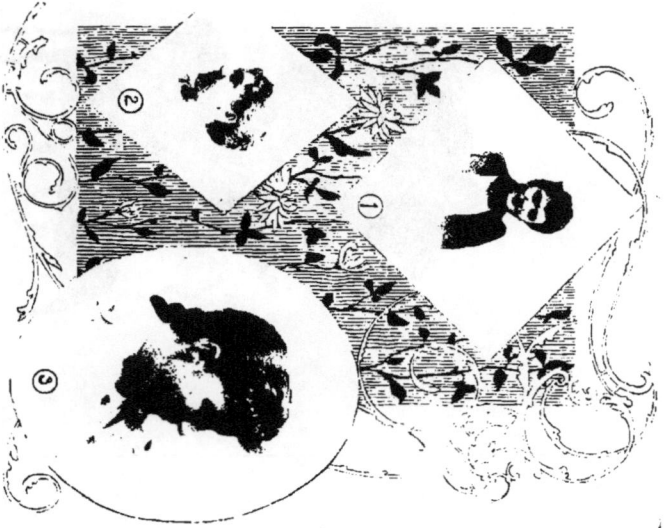

JOHN R. DICKENS CAMP NO. 341, SARDIS, MISS.

1 MISS BESSIE TAYLOR HUNTER, SPONSOR, SARDIS, MISS.
2 MISS BLANCHE TAYLOR, MAID OF HONOR.
3 MISS LONA WALTON, " "

GHOLSON CAMP, ABERDEEN, MISS.

1 MISS ANNIE LOWE JONAS, SPONSOR, ABERDEEN, MISS.
2 MISS KATHARINE ALLEN, MAID OF HONOR.
3 MISS INDIA ROGERS SYKES, " "
4 MISS JULIA JONAS JORDAN, " "
5 MISS MARY IMOGENE SMITH, " "

WALTER L. KEIRN CAMP NO. 398, LEXINGTON, MISS.

1 MISS MAY KATE BAKER, SPONSOR, LEXINGTON, MISS.
2 MISS AMMA BEALL, MAID OF HONOR.
3 MISS MALIE WYATT, " "

CONF'D HIST. ASS'N CAMP NO. 28, MEMPHIS, TENN.

1 MISS AIDA R. HEAD, SPONSOR, HOUSTON, TEXAS.
2 MISS PAULINE M. CRAWLEY, MAID OF HONOR.
3 LORA A. EIDSON, " "

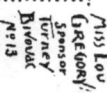

TEXAS ENG. CO. DESM.

1 MISS JOSIE STEELE, Sponsor, S. H. Stout Camp No. 583, Eastland. Texas.

2 MISS JENNIE WEBB, Sponsor, John G. Walker Camp No. 128, Madison-ville, Texas.

4 MISS CLARA TRAMMELL, Sponsor, J. E. Johnston Camp No. 78, Sher-man, Texas.

3 MISS MAIDA McLEOD, Houston, Texas, Maid of Honor to Miss Clara Trammell.

5 MISS MAGGIE A. EASTERLING, Sponsor, Jones Co. Camp No. 612. Anson, Texas.

6 MISS ELIZABETH DARI, Sponsor, Standvatie Camp No. 573, Chelsea. Ind. Ter.

7 MISS IRENE BRADLEY, Sponsor, S. E. Texas Div., Fairfield, Texas.

8 MISS MABEL CLAIRE DURST, Sponsor, R. S. Gould Camp No. 611, Jewett, Texas.

9 MISS FALBY HYMAN, Sponsor, Hampton Camp No. 450, Florence, S. C.

10 MISS HETTIE E. STRICKLAND, Sponsor, W. N. Pendleton Camp No. 579, Deport, Texas.

JUNIUS DANIEL CAMP No. 336, LITTLETON, N. C.

1 MISS CLAUDIA ATHERTON JOHNSTON,
SPONSOR,
LITTLETON, NORTH CAROLINA.

2 MISS AVA LONG FLEMING, MAID OF HONOR.
3 MISS KATHARINE H. LEACH, "   "
4 MISS SUSIE IRVING JOHNSTON, "   "
5 MISS MARY WHITNELL THORNE, MAID OF HONOR.
6 MISS ANNIE WILLIAMS PIERCE, "   "

ANDREW COLEMAN CAMP NO. 301, BRYSON CITY, N. C.

" MISS NORA T. EVERETT, SPONSOR, BRYSON CITY, N. C.
1 MISS BENDIE PENDER, MAID OF HONOR.
2 MISS LILA ARTHUR, " "
3 MISS SALLIE BATTLE, " "
4 MISS MAUD DAVIS, " "
5 MISS FANNIE EVERETT,

1 MISS HETTIE WILKINS, Maid of Honor to Washington Camp No 239, Brenham, Texas.
2 MISS KATIE B. BRICKEN, Maid of Honor to Gracy Camp No. 472, Luverne, Ala.
3 MISS ELIZABETH L. SCOTT, Ewell, Va., Maid of Honor to Miss M. A. Jones.
4 MISS VIRGINIA T. ARMISTEAD, Williamsburg, Va., Maid of Honor to Miss M. A. Jones.

Miss Margaret Waring.
CHARLESTON, S. C.
State Sponsor for South Carolina.

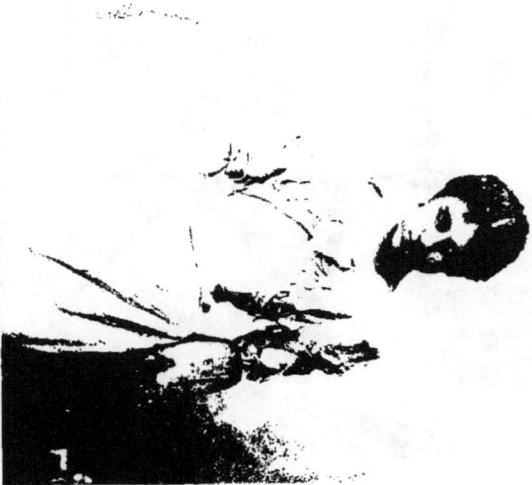

Miss Ada Lee Thompson.
LITTLE ROCK, ARK.
State Sponsor for Arkansas.

JOHN F. HILL CAMP No. 27, CLARKSVILLE, ARK.

1 MISS LILLIAN WARD HILL, SPONSOR,
            CLARKSVILLE, ARK.

2 MISS SUSIE McCONNELL,   MAID OF HONOR.
3 MISS LOUISE BROWN,   "
4 MISS JENNETT PENNINGTON, "   "

5 MISS JESSIE CRAVENS, MAID OF HONOR.
6 MISS ALICE HICKS,   "   "

HEAD QUARTERS. A.N.V.

APRIL 10 1865

General Order No 9.

After four years of arduous service, marked by unsurpassed courage and fortitude, the Army of Northern Virginia has been compelled to yield to overwhelming numbers and resources.

I need not tell the brave survivors of so many hard fought battles, who have remained steadfast to the last, that I have consented to this result from no distrust of them. But feeling that valor and devotion could accomplish nothing that would compensate for the loss that must have attended the continuation of the contest, I determined to avoid the useless sacrifice of those whose past services have endeared them to their countrymen.

By the terms of agreement officers and men can return to their homes and remain until exchanged.

You will take with you the satisfaction that proceeds from the consciousness of duty faithfully performed; and I earnestly pray that a merciful God will extend to you His blessing and protection.

With an unceasing admiration of your constancy and devotion to your country, and a grateful remembrance of your kind and generous consideration of myself, I bid you an affectionate farewell.

R. E. Lee, General.

DEANE

The Photographer

FORT WORTH, DALLAS, WACO,
HOUSTON AND GALVESTON,
TEXAS . . . . . .

UNRIVALED FOR EXCELLENCE OF WORK.

MANY OF THE HANDSOMEST ENGRAVINGS
IN THIS VOLUME WERE MADE FROM
PHOTOGRAPHS BY

DEANE